Victorian &
Edwardian
Hampshire

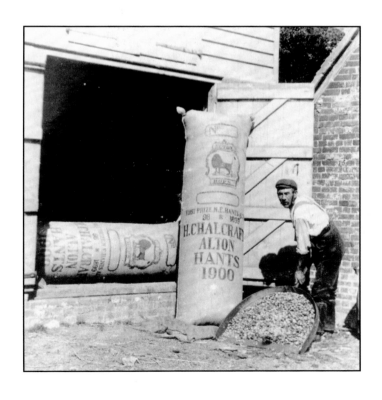

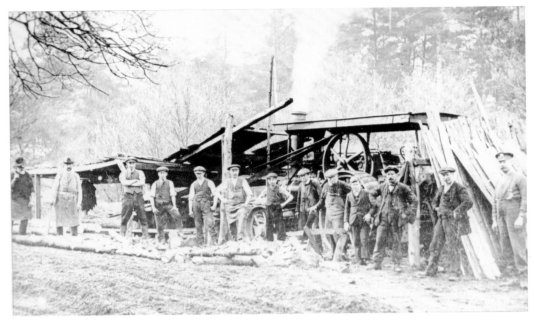

BRAMSHILL PARK

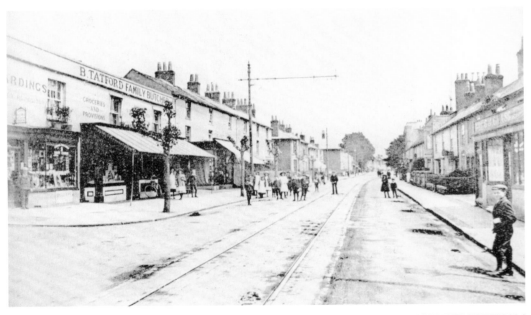

WEST STREET, FAREHAM

Victorian &
Edwardian
Hampshire

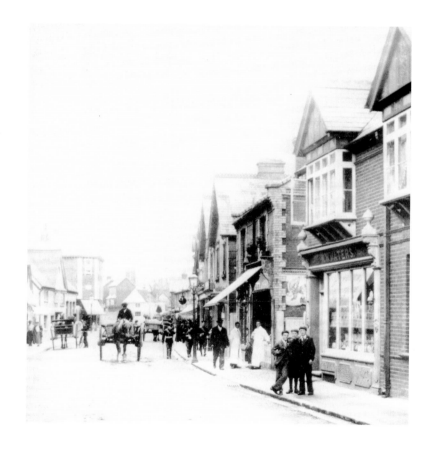

Barry Stapleton

AMBERLEY

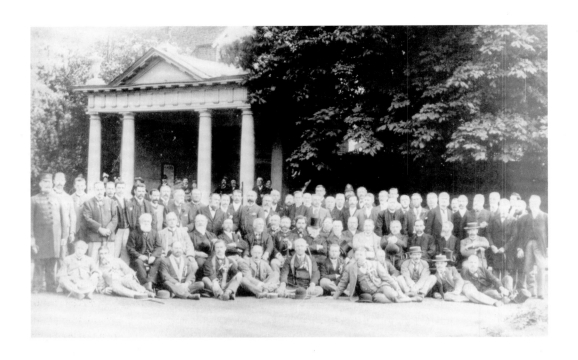

First published 1993 under the title *Hampshire of 100 Years Ago*
This revised edition first published 2008

Amberley Publishing
Cirencester Road, Chalford,
Stroud, Gloucestershire, GL6 8PE

British Library Cataloguing in Publication Data.
A catalogue record for this book is available from the British Library.

ISBN 978-1-84868-028-9

Typesetting and origination by Amberley Publishing
Printed in Great Britain by Amberley Publishing

PREFACE

This book is not intended to provide a comprehensive survey of Hampshire at the end of the nineteenth century and the beginning of the twentieth. Nor is it just a pretty picture book. It would have been comparatively easy to have produced such a volume for there are many surviving photographs from around a century ago that show the beauty of the county at that time. However, this book concentrates on the people of Hampshire. Not the rich and powerful resplendent on their country estates and in their mansions, but ordinary men, women and children who lived frequently harsh lives, always close to poverty, and with the constant fear of being brought up 'on the parish' or the dread of being confined to the workhouse.

For most of the people, if they survived the early hazards of infancy—a man or woman's expectation of life at birth was only in the mid-forties—there was to be a life of unremitting labour, frequently poorly paid, so that they could afford few pleasures to enhance their lives and relieve the monotony of the daily tasks. The harshness of life was exacerbated in the late nineteenth century by economic depression in both agriculture and industry. The second half of the nineteenth century had seen the number of farm workers decline substantially as mechanization was introduced, but they still formed the majority of the work-force in northern and central Hampshire. However, the opening up of the prairies of North America by the expansion of railways was to bring cheap grain to Britain and reduce the acreage of grain crops grown by arable farmers, and the development of refrigeration brought increasing supplies of cheaper frozen meat from Argentina to the detriment of pastoral farmers, hence even more pressure to reduce the agricultural work-force, both in number and relative wealth, was created.

At least in Hampshire, unlike many rural counties, it was possible to move to the southern coastal part of the county in search of alternative employment since Southampton was the expanding terminus for trans-Atlantic liners, while Eastleigh became the growing centre for the London and South Western Railway Company's carriage and wagon works, transferred from London in the late 1880s. Bournemouth required increasing numbers of domestic servants as it emerged as the county's most fashionable resort in competition with Southsea, the later

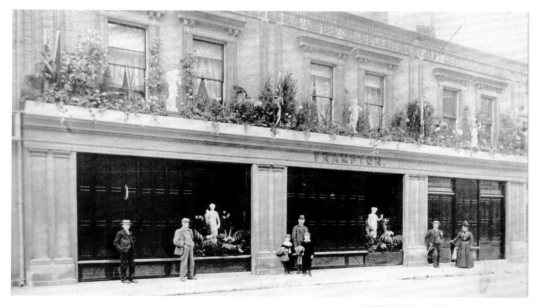

JEWRY STREET, WINCHESTER

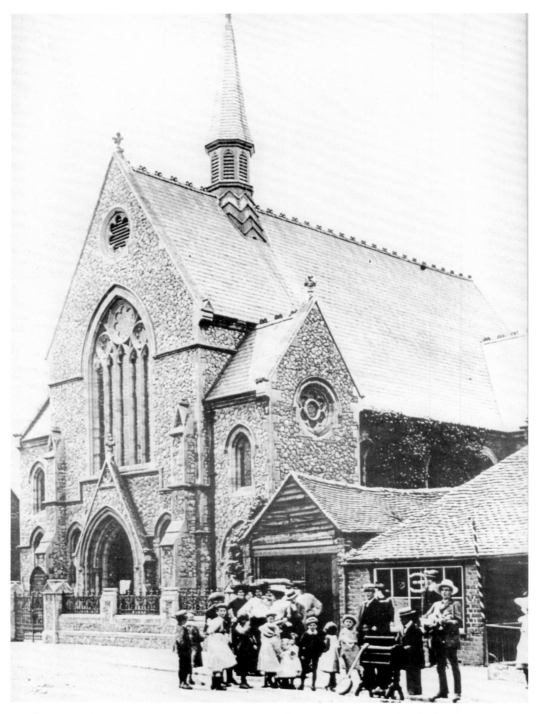

NORTH STREET, HAVANT

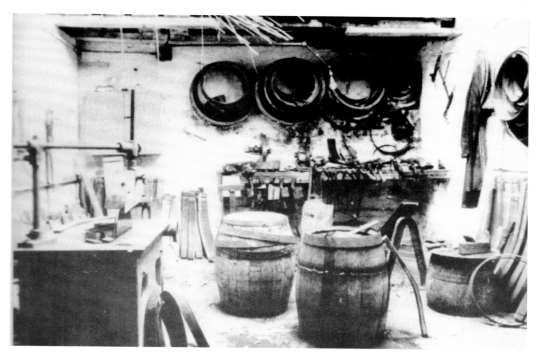

COOPERAGE, GALE'S BREWERY, HORNDEAN

nineteenth-century seaside suburb of Portsmouth, which itself could provide other not very highly paid work in a naval dockyard of considerable size. Naval requirements spilled over from Portsmouth harbour leading to the growth of employment in Gosport. It was the rise of Britain as the late nineteenth century's foremost world power that necessitated both naval and military forces to be transported to actual or potential trouble spots.

Despite the provision of much-needed employment the environment in which many of the urban men and women had to dwell was not always attractive, the row upon row of nineteenth-century terraced houses and the infilling of courts producing slum conditions inappropriate to the raising of the large numbers of children that late Victorian families tended to have. Thus many of these youngsters began life in benighted and deprived circumstances, born into families under considerable economic and social stress, the effects of which can be seen in the volume of suicide cases reported in the pages of the *Hampshire Telegraph* of one hundred years ago. Life for children, however, was generally much harder than today, whether born in town or country. School, in which corporal punishment was frequent, would last a few short years interspersed with the precedence of casual work or domestic requirements, and many boys by the age of ten were in fulltime employment, while their sisters of similar age could find themselves engaged in long hours of domestic service.

The homes of these poor families would have contained little in the way of material possessions—those they did own would be old and worn. Food was an equally scarce commodity, bread and potatoes forming the greater portion of the diet. Many small children went to school having not eaten at all, what food there had been in the house being consumed by

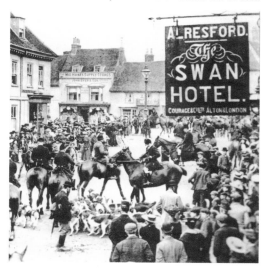

THE HUNT, ALRESFORD

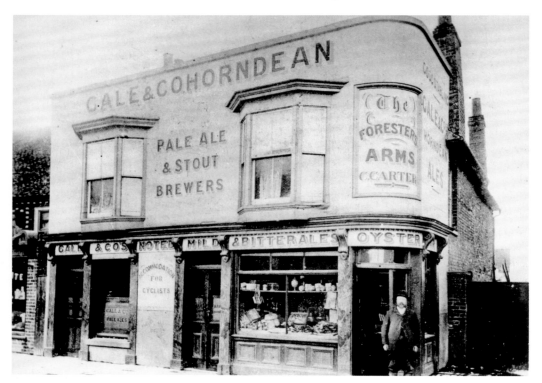

NORTH STREET, HAVANT

the father before his day's toil as the breadwinner, assuming that he was employed. Much work, unfortunately, was casual and hence not guaranteed. As a consequence the very poorest families were unable to obtain credit at the local shop, which acquired its groceries loose in bulk and weighed them out before pouring them into bags of differing shapes, sizes and colours to be sold to individual customers.

The better-off aspiring middle class, a growing and increasingly influential group in nineteenth-century England, dressed more fashionably, had time for leisure and entertainment, hence the growth of Bournemouth and Southsea, and attended church or chapel, both of which played significant parts in their social lives. As a larger proportion of the population rose in status so the gap between them and the poor widened. Their homes would have more furniture and carpets, more clothes and shoes and their larders would be stocked with the increasingly imported foods such as meat, fruit, dairy produce, grain and wines and spirits.

Unfortunately, in the late nineteenth century almost all photography was carried on outdoors so interiors of houses, except occasionally for those of the very rich, are rare. Thus this book is illustrated almost entirely with views of our ancestors mainly at work, outside their houses, in their communities, shopping, enjoying leisure or celebrations.

Photographers, generally, looked for views and places which seemed attractive, tending to avoid the less desirable areas. Hence these snapshots of a moment in history do not always tell the whole truth of the hard life led by many a hundred years ago.

Hampshire has probably been inhabited for nearly a quarter of a million years, archaeological evidence indicating that man has exploited the county's resources for something approaching that time span. In the old (palaeolithic) and middle (mesolithic) Stone Ages man was a nomadic hunter-gatherer and theoretically signs of his presence could exist anywhere in the county. In practice, the known sites of early man's habitation fall mainly into two groups: those along the coast where man could have exploited the resources of both sea and land, and those on hilltops, which provided more easily defensible locations. However, these represent only those dwelling places that have been discovered and there could be many more remaining to be unearthed. Hilltop sites have been explored because they have remained largely undeveloped by modern man, whereas coastal areas subjected to recent development have also provided archaeological evidence of early habitation. Where urban growth has taken place over the last few hundred years, however, evidence of early man's possible presence has remained hidden.

With the coming of the Iron Age and the development of iron-tipped coulters for ploughing, it is probable that man was able to till not just the lighter soils of the chalk downs, but also some of the heavier ones away from the hilltops. As a result the population would have been more widely dispersed in the county, a process that may have continued throughout Roman and Anglo-Saxon times, although much settlement remained on previously inhabited sites.

It was in AD 43 that the Romans established themselves in Hampshire, where their presence was a peaceful one. The most important settlements were *Calleva Atrebatum* (Silchester) in the north of the county, *Venta Belgarum* (Winchester) in the centre and the port of *Clausmatum* (Bitterne) in the south, but the county was dotted with villas to administer the farming activities of the mainly British population. Since the Roman presence lasted nearly four centuries (the equivalent of a span of time back to the first Queen Elizabeth from today) it is no surprise that they became integrated with the local population. In the last century of Roman occupation the shores of south-east England were frequently raided by Saxons, resulting in the building of a series of defensive sites of which *Portus Adurni* (Portchester) was a fine example of Roman fortification.

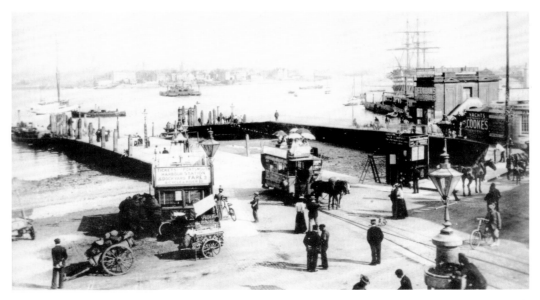

GOSPORT

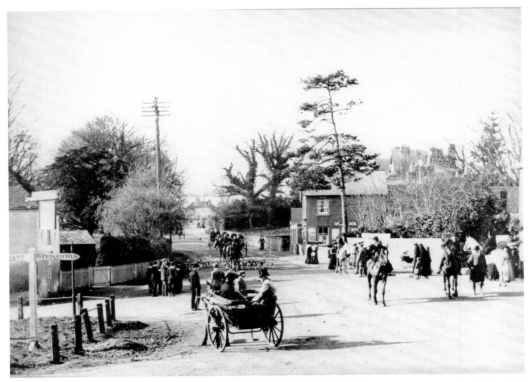

HORNDEAN

However, with the barbarian attacks on the Roman empire in the early fifth century, Roman soldiers were withdrawn from Britain and by the middle of that century all contact with Rome ceased. Increasingly the south coast of England was subjected to invasion by Angles, Saxons and Jutes and by the end of the century the Saxon kingdom of Wessex, of which Hampshire was a part, was founded. The Saxons settled in new villages along the river valleys, being mainly involved in farming and forest clearance. Generally they avoided the Roman villas and towns, *Calleva* appearing to have been deserted. During more than five centuries of Saxon domination, Roman organization was replaced by new administration, King Ine of Wessex (688–726) issuing his own code of laws; and the conversion of Hampshire to Christianity took place in the seventh century, the bishopric being established at Winchester about AD 676. There the Old Minster church had been built by the king of the West Saxons and this royal patronage meant that the Anglo-Saxon church in Hampshire became one of the wealthiest dioceses in England. Winchester thus retained its importance as a town, now with royal connections, so much so that in the eleventh century it became the capital of Anglo-Saxon England. Meanwhile, a trading settlement at the mouth of the Itchen grew into the urban centre Hamtun, which became the fortified town of Southampton.

Saxon rule came to an end with the conquest of England by William, Duke of Normandy in 1066. A Norman aristocracy generally replaced the Anglo-Saxon one, and Norman-French was the spoken language of the new administration, although the Hampshire peasants and poorer residents of the towns continued to speak in English. New Norman landowners took over Hampshire estates and, with a flourishing trade developing with France, Southampton grew in importance. With a strong central government and relative peace the population of the county, as in the rest of England, grew during the twelfth and thirteenth centuries. There were, however, periods of civil disturbance between barons and monarch. These were not terminated in June 1215 when King John rode from his castle at Odiham to seal the Magna Carta at Runnymede for, in the following year, disaffected barons appealed to the king of France for help. The result was that an army of 7,000 men swept through southern England, arriving at Winchester on 14 June to find it in flames, moved on to capture Portchester castle, and finally obtained the surrender of Odiham. No doubt for the people of Hampshire a marauding army was a particularly unwelcome

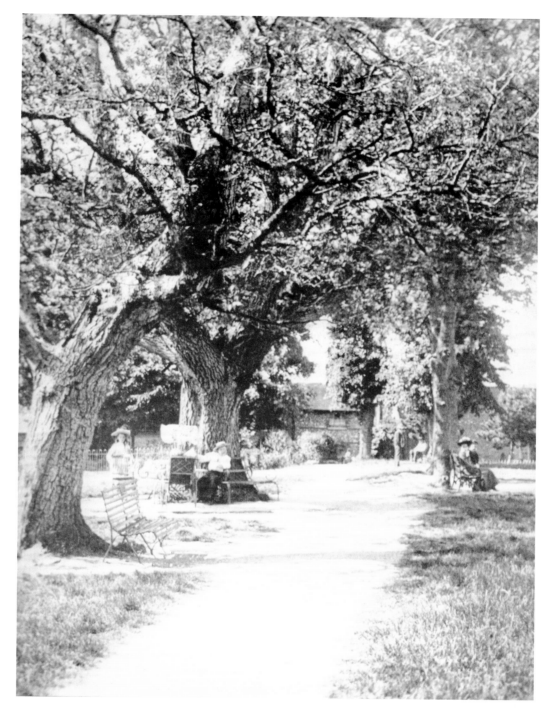

RECREATION GROUND, ANDOVER

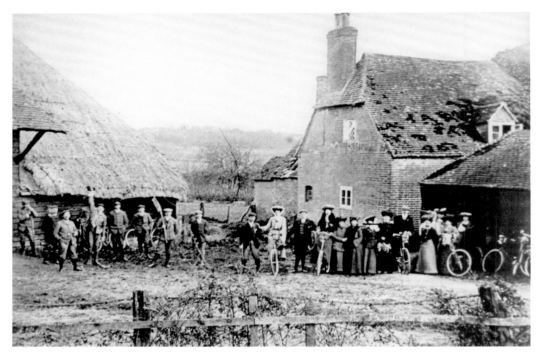

TITCHFIELD

sight, especially in the summer months when much damage to growing crops could have ensued.

Fifty years later the county was to be host to the army of Simon de Montfort. Following his defeat of Henry III's forces at Lewes in May 1264, Simon called the first representative parliament in 1265 and, after a settlement between the king and barons was reached, the de Montfort family and followers spent Easter at Odiham. There they ate well, but for many of the ordinary local people poverty was widespread, for 800 poor were fed on that Christian festival. Clearly the problems of rising prices and growing population were having some serious effects on living standards.

Increasingly, in the late thirteenth and early fourteenth centuries, bad harvests brought higher death rates as insufficient food was available, culminating in the disastrous harvests of 1314–16 that caused famine, disease and death throughout western Europe. The pressure of population on economic resources was finally removed by the arrival in 1348–9 of the Black Death. Millions died in Europe and probably one-third to almost a half of the population of Britain succumbed. In Hampshire, as elsewhere, some places suffered more severely, others less. Bishop's Waltham lost 65 per cent of its tenants and Titchfield a massive 80 per cent. The return of further plague epidemics in 1361–2, 1369 and 1374–5 must have reduced Hampshire's population still further, creating increasing problems of labour shortage—as evidenced at Highclere where only fifteen per cent of labour services were performed in 1376. The declining number of agricultural workers meant many Hampshire landlords could not find sufficient labour to cultivate their lands; the feudal system was breaking apart. Based on the provision of labour services by unfree peasants to powerful landlords, the system was unable to cope with serious labour shortages, thus increasingly landlords converted from direct farming to rental leasing of the land to tenant farmers. Given that the plague remained nationally endemic, the population of the country remained low for much of the first half of the fifteenth century so that a decline of perhaps some 60 per cent of the national population had taken place between the 1340s and the 1440s, and most peasants by the latter decade had become tenant farmers, not feudal vassals. Urban centres also suffered and Winchester was said to have nearly 1,000 empty houses by 1450.

As a result of these changes living standards rose for those families that had survived the ravages of the plague. More land became available for them, the wages of urban labourers increased, and in England a flourishing woollen textile industry developed so that the previous exports of raw wool from ports like Southampton to the

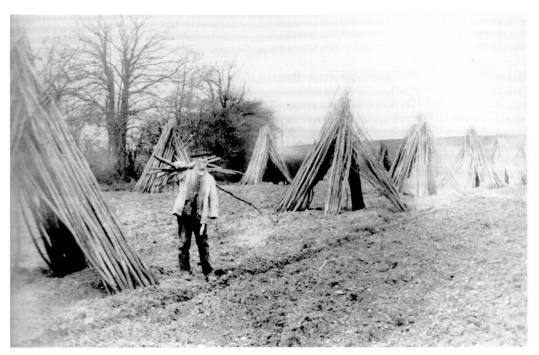

STACKING HOP POLES, ALTON

northern Italian textile manufacturing towns were replaced by exports of unfinished manufactured high quality woollen cloths. Unfortunately, from Southampton's viewpoint, most of this export went from London. Hence the medieval communities of French and Italian merchants began to decline along with Southampton's commercial fortunes in the sixteenth century.

By then, in Tudor times, the flourishing textile industry was well established in both the small towns and countryside of northern Hampshire, taking advantage of the large number of sheep grazing on the thin, chalky soil of the downs. Many peasants thus had alternative employment in spinning and weaving to supplement earnings from the land, particularly when the seasonal nature of farming left many underemployed. These earnings were to be particularly important during Elizabeth I's reign, since by then the population of the country reached once more its pre-Black Death level and continued to grow during the early seventeenth century. This pressure of population on resources caused considerable inflation and consequent increasing levels of poverty among the peasants, with many dependent on poor law doles and charitable relief. Since large farmers and merchants with goods to sell at inflated prices grew richer, so the gap between rich and poor widened. Wage earners fared badly with their real incomes being halved. Rising population also meant unemployment and with political and religious uncertainties associated with the Reformation and counter-Reformation, there were many problems facing the men and women of Hampshire.

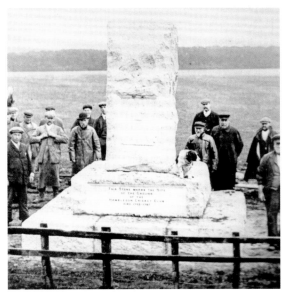

CRICKET MEMORIAL, HAMBLEDON

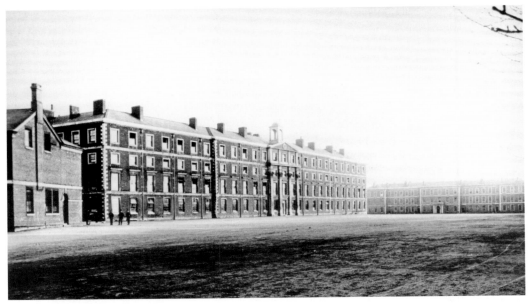

BARRACKS, WINCHESTER

At the end of the period of inflation these problems were exacerbated by civil war, which divided local communities and the county gentry alike. There were no clear divisions, but Winchester remained loyal to the Crown whereas both Southampton and Portsmouth were supporters of Parliament. The Puritan Fathers had not been unwelcome in Southampton when they had sailed in 1620 and many Hampshire folk opposed the Crown

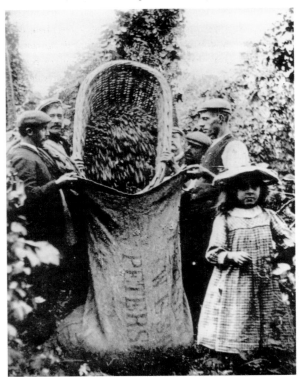

HOP MEASURING, PETERSFIELD

for religious reasons. Some important families like the Paulets of Basing House supported the king whereas Sir William Waller, a cousin of John Paulet, Marquess of Winchester, was a Parliamentary general. The Tichbornes and the Sandys of the Vyne favoured the king, whereas the Flemings of North Stoneham and the Nortons of Southwick supported Parliament. At Hursley Richard Major's daughter, Dorothy, married Oliver Cromwell's son, Richard. Battles occurred at Cheriton in 1644 where the Royalists were defeated. Winchester fell to Cromwell in 1645 and Basing House, after two years under siege, surrendered shortly after Cromwell's arrival. For many of the ordinary people of Hampshire the end of the war must have meant much relief from marauding bands from Basing House, from armies marching over their lands, and from soldiers being billeted upon them.

The second half of the seventeenth century was a less turbulent period and one in which, following the restoration of the Stuart monarchy in 1660 came their departure in 1688. The

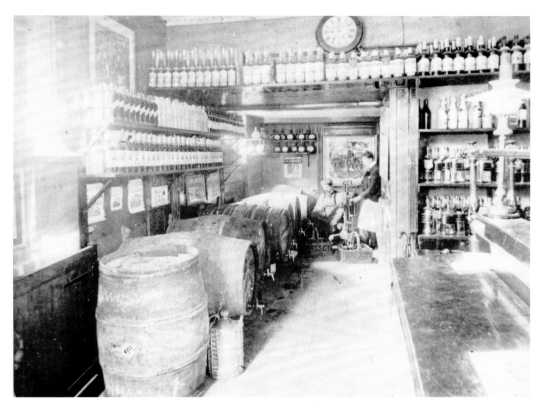

PRESTON WATSON, NORTH STREET, HAVANT

arrival of William of Orange to the English throne was followed by a period of political stability. For Hampshire people there were also better times. Population growth slowed substantially and this, combined with agricultural improvements raising yields per acre, meant that a surplus of grain was produced. Thus bread and ale became cheaper and living standards could rise. Although Southampton continued to be in comparative economic decline, Portsmouth began its rise as a naval port and by the early eighteenth century contained a dockyard employing over 2,000 men—probably the largest single unit in Britain, or even anywhere in the world, since this was decades before the Industrial Revolution. In northern Hampshire, however, the old established woollen textile industry was in serious decline in the later seventeenth century, unable to compete with the specialist producers in East Anglia and especially west Yorkshire.

The countryside was being increasingly altered by enclosure, which changed the open fields of medieval times and allowed for improvements in crop rotation with turnips, swedes and clover, rye grass and sainfoin being introduced. The eighteenth century saw the rise of large landowners, tenant farmers and landless agricultural labourers. In the later decades of that century rapid population growth and war with France caused prices to rise substantially so that once again increasing problems of poverty were experienced, especially among the agricultural labourers of Hampshire whose work was beginning to be affected by mechanization, with the appearance of the first threshing machines by the end of the century.

The end of the war with France in 1815 brought an economic depression especially in agriculture but also in some industries, in particular those associated with the war effort. Thus Portsmouth and Gosport were both affected by unemployment. Bankruptcies in farming were followed by riots against machinery and the burning of ricks. Repressive measures were taken with the imprisonment and transportation for life of farm labourers. The escalating costs of poverty led to changes in the treatment of the poor, the harsher new Poor Law being introduced in 1834. There was no consideration of the real causes: the population was growing faster than employment opportunities, government policies or trade cycles—the poor were regarded as indigent and feckless

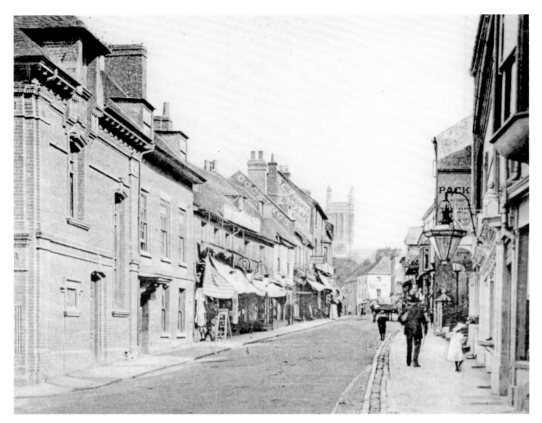

HIGH STREET, ANDOVER

and to be treated accordingly despite the evidence of growing hardship being unavoidable.

The nineteenth century was to witness continual population growth and also remarkable industrial and commercial expansion, with the coming of the railways enhancing the trend but at the same time leading to the decline and disappearance of markets and fairs in some of Hampshire's smaller towns, which were bypassed by the railway lines. However, these were more than offset by the expansion of coastal resorts, particularly Southsea and in the ancient parish of Holdenhurst, the fashionable centre of Bournemouth. In addition the London and South Western Railway Company moved its carriage and wagon works from Nine Elms to Bishopstoke, where the railway town of Eastleigh was created. In the north-east of the county the establishment of the military town of Aldershot was made possible by the railway with the assistance of the Basingstoke Canal.

Increasingly the population was becoming mobile over greater distances, and its vast expansion (for example, the population of Portsea Island rose from 33,000 in 1801 to 186,000 in 1901—over 560 per cent) meant a rising demand for accommodation. This led to an expanding brick-making industry at Fareham. Similarly the growth of Southampton led to brick-works at Chandlers Ford. The nineteenth century was to see the resurgence of Southampton, again heavily influenced by the arrival of the railway, as a great commercial port noted for its provision of trans-Atlantic passenger services.

Much of the urban growth was in cheap housing without adequate water or sanitation, leading to outbreaks of typhoid and cholera in what quickly became slums. As the population continued its inexorable rise, the Church created new parishes and built churches accordingly. By 1918 Portsmouth and Southsea had nineteen new parishes, Southampton sixteen and Bournemouth fourteen, and the number of parishes in the county had nearly doubled over the previous hundred years. Similarly the number of schools increased. The county already had grammar schools and a number of villages had schools supported by the local Anglican church or Dissenting chapel. After the 1870 Elementary Education Act, Board schools were established throughout the county and

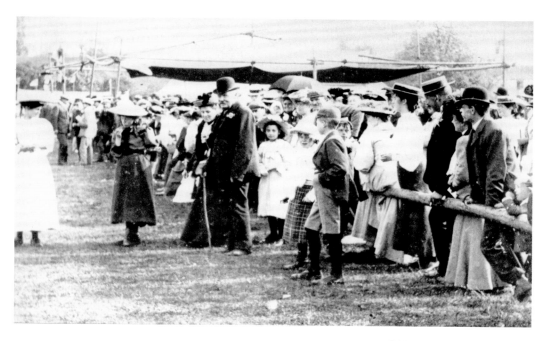

COUNTRY FAIR, YATELEY

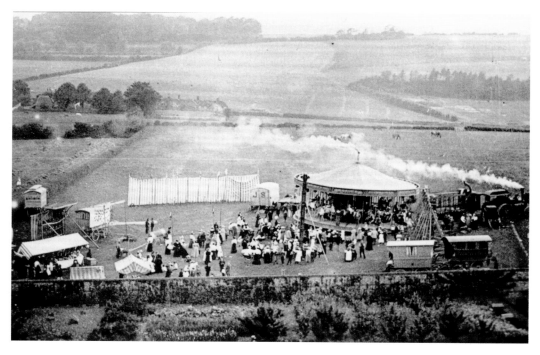

FAIRGROUND

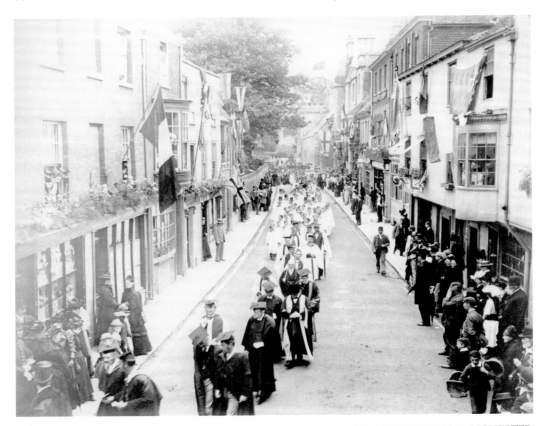

COLLEGE STREET, WINCHESTER

Hampshire County Council, formed in 1889, took responsibility for the administration of education, the reform of local government being one of the greatest of the changes affecting the county in the last century.

With the onset of international competition in the late nineteenth century the British economy began to fall from its position of supremacy, gained by the fact that Britain was the first country to industrialize. The competition was felt first in agriculture where, despite the introduction of machinery resulting in fewer agricultural workers being employed, foreign grain was still cheaper partly because of the vast scale of production and mechanization on the North American prairies and the availability of cheaper transport. Britain had exported railways throughout the world and this meant grain could reach ports more quickly and cheaply, and improvements in world shipping brought down freight costs. British grain farmers, including those in Hampshire, could not compete. Worse was to follow since refrigerated ships meant foreign meat could be imported frozen and more cheaply, first from the vast plains of Argentina and then from Australia. By the end of the century the United States and Germany had overhauled Britain in the output of steel and coal also. Furthermore, Britain was not at the forefront of new developments—electricity, chemicals and communications were all being expanded faster either in America or Europe. The First World War exacerbated matters, firstly by protecting outdated industries for longer, and secondly by converting Britain from a large creditor to a large debtor nation. One of Britain's problems was that many of the world's new and important materials were not part of her natural resources—oil, rubber and aluminium, for example, had to be imported.

The first two were particularly important since there was to be a major expansion of motor transport through the German development of the internal combustion engine. Gradually the roads of Hampshire were to see rising numbers of vehicles so that men with flags walking ahead became redundant. This placed a major strain on roads meant only for horse-drawn traffic; thus one significant change was the building of new roads, not always to the benefit of the countryside. More recently this has been illustrated by the demonstrations at Twyford Down, near

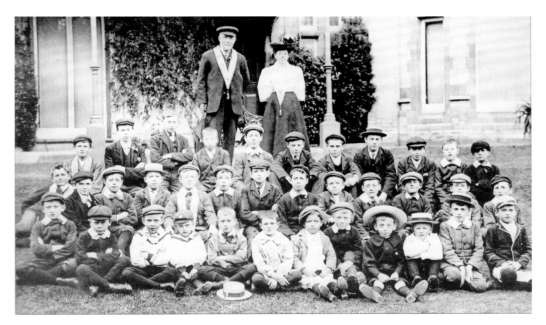

BISHOPSTOKE

Winchester. Associated with this growth of personal transport has been the need to construct more and more car parking facilities in major towns while the number of railways has declined, as demonstrated by the Meon Valley line. Because motor transport needed oil, the county saw the development of a major refinery at Fawley dominating the water's edge west of Southampton.

As the proportion of the population in Hampshire's villages fell, so that of its coastal towns and their hinterlands rose. The areas inland of Portsmouth and Southampton became heavily developed, with an almost continuous ribbon north of Portsmouth from Emsworth in the east to Fareham in the west and also north to Clanfield, most of these residents travelling to work by car. Similarly the Southampton conurbation stretched from Totton in the west to the Hamble river and north to Chandlers Ford. Basingstoke was heavily developed, swallowing villages to the west, as were the Farnborough, Aldershot and Farnham areas in the north-east of the county. It could be said that the motor car has much to answer for. Nevertheless, one development is heavily dependent on motor transport—the county's growing tourist industry. Increasing numbers of visitors from both home and abroad are being encouraged to enjoy not only the history and heritage of the towns, but also the countryside, much of which remains unspoilt. The Iron Age hilltop site of Old Winchester Hill still remains a place of tranquil beauty where man can stand where his ancestors did in prehistoric times. Meanwhile, not far away in Portsmouth, visitors can compare Henry VIII's Southsea Castle

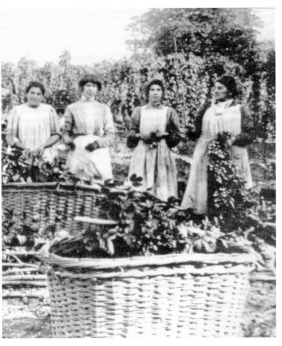

HOP PICKING, ODIHAM

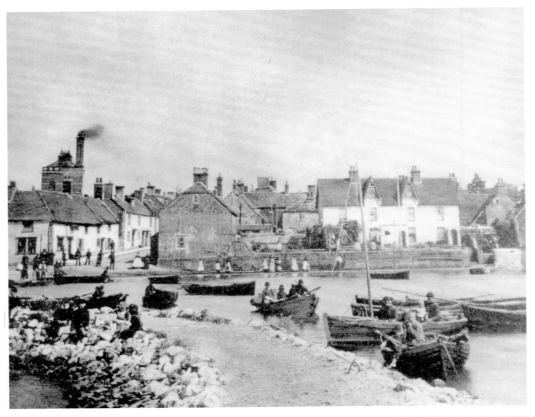

THE QUAY, EMSWORTH

with the neighbouring D-Day museum of the late twentieth century and then turn to see warships of the sixteenth, eighteenth and nineteenth centuries—respectively the *Mary Rose*, *Victory* and *Warrior*—in the dockyard, now substantially reduced to a repair facility. Perhaps seeing the artefacts of previous wars as tourist attractions is better than fighting future ones, as the residents of Portsmouth and Southampton, blitzed in the Second World War, would no doubt agree.

All of these tourist developments, from the New Forest to marinas like Ocean Village and Port Solent, and the emergence of a second Hampshire University at Portsmouth to join that in Southampton, indicates the rising living standards of Hampshire folk in the twentieth century. There are, even so, those who do not share in this wealth, usually the unemployed and the old. In comparison to their forebears of one hundred years ago, who had nowhere near enough mobility or wealth to help them experience wider opportunities for personal development, as many of the photographs and accounts in this volume testify, late twentieth-century Hampshire residents are more fortunate. In another hundred years time, when the twenty-first century is drawing to its close, those then alive will look back to our time in this county and think themselves fortunate that they live four generations later.

Barry Stapleton

Victorian & Edwardian Hampshire

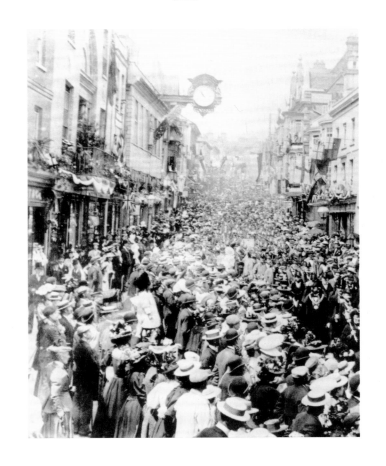

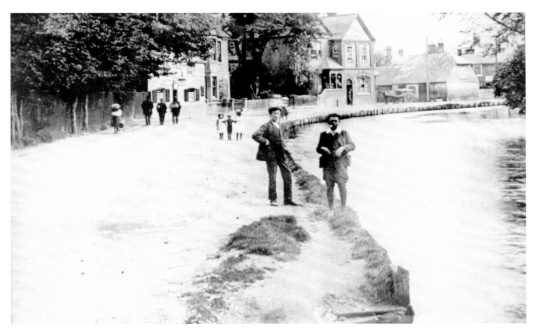

CHURCH LANE, BISHOPSTOKE

RIVERSIDE VILLAGES

There are no more refreshing places in Hampshire, one might almost say in England, than the green level valleys of the Test and Itchen that wind, alternately widening and narrowing. through the downland country to Southampton Water. Twin rivers they may be called, flowing at no great distance apart through the same kind of country, and closely alike in their general features: land and water intermixed—greenest, water-meadows and crystal currents that divide and subdivide and join again, and again separate, forming many a miniature island and long slip of wet meadow with streams on either side. At all times refreshing to the sight and pleasant to dwell by, they are best 'when it is summer and the green is deep'.

They are not long rivers—the Test and Itchen—but long enough for men with unfevered blood in their veins to find sweet and peaceful homes on their margins. I think I know quite a dozen villages on the former stream, and fifteen or sixteen on the latter, in any one of which I could spend long years in perfect contentment. There are towns, too, ancient Romsey and Winchester, and modern hideous Eastleigh; but the little centres are best to live in. These are, indeed, among the most characteristic Hampshire villages; mostly small, with old thatched cottages, unlike, yet harmonizing, irregularly placed along the roadside; each with its lovely walls set among gaily coloured flowers; the farm with its rural sounds and smells, its big horses and milch-cows led and driven along the quiet streets; the small ancient church with its low, square tower, or grey shingled spire; and great trees standing singly or in groups or rows—oak and elm and ash; and often some ivy-grown relic of antiquity—ivy, indeed, everywhere. The charm of these villages that look as natural and one with the scene as chalk down and trees and green meadows, and have an air of immemorial quiet and a human life that is part of nature's life, unstrenuous, slow and sweet, has not yet been greatly disturbed. It is not here as in some parts of Hampshire, and as it is pretty well everywhere in Surrey, that most favoured county, the Xanadu of the mighty ones of the money-market, where they oftenest decree their lordly pleasure domes. Those vast red-brick habitations of the Kubla Khans of the city which stare and glare at you from all openings in pine woods, across wide heaths and commons, and from hill-sides and hilltops, produce the idea that they were turned out complete at some stupendous manufactory of houses at a distance, and sent out by the hundred to be set up wherever wanted, and where they are almost always utterly out of keeping with their surroundings, and consequently a blot on and a disfigurement of the landscape.

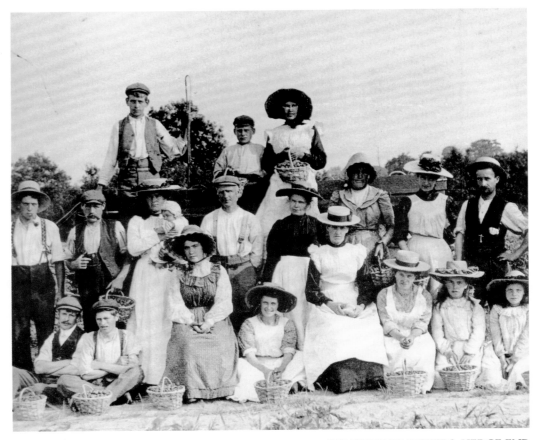

STRAWBERRY PICKERS, HEDGE END

Happily the downland slopes overlooking these green valleys have so far been neglected by the class of persons who live in mansions; for the time being they are ours, and by 'ours' I mean all those who love and reverence this earth. But which of the two is best I cannot say. One prefers the Test and another the Itchen, doubtless because in a matter of this kind the earth-lover will invariably prefer the spot he knows most intimately; and for this reason, much as I love the Test, long as I would linger by it, I love the Itchen more, having had a closer intimacy with it. I dare say that some of my friends, old Wykehamists, who as boys caught their first trout close by the ancient sacred city and have kept up their acquaintance with its crystal currents, will laugh at me for writing as I do. But there are places, as there are faces, which draw the soul, and with which, in a little while, one becomes strangely intimate.

W. H. Hudson

THE STRAWBERRY SEASON

During the last two or three weeks, enormous quantities of strawberries have been sent to the London and provincial market from Swanswick, Bursledon, Botley, and neighbourhood, thousands upon thousands of the now familiar cross-handled baskets having been dealt with by the Waterloo officials in that time. Some idea of the traffic may be gathered from the fact that on one morning no fewer than sixty pair-horse vans were required to cart the fruit to various London markets, the amount of labour involved in checking and making out accounts severely testing the parcel department staff at that station.

Hampshire Telegraph, 14 July 1894

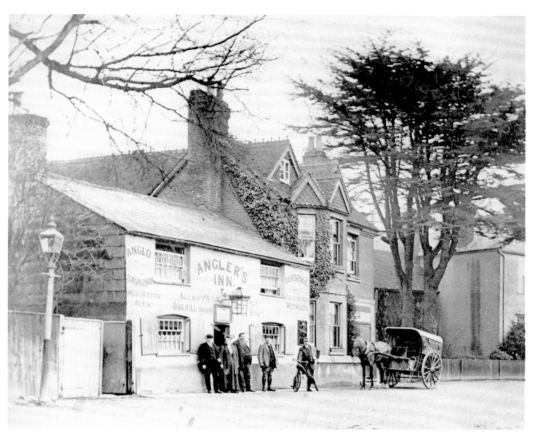

ANGLER'S INN, BISHOPSTOKE

WHITE HORSE INN

Who now used these roads except myself,
A market wagon every other Wednesday,
A solitary tramp, some very fresh one
Ignorant of these eleven houseless miles,
A motorist from a distance slowing down
To taste whatever luxury he can
In having North Downs clear behind, South clear
before,
And being midway between two railway lines
Far out of sight or sound of them? There are
Some houses—down the by-lanes; and a few
Are visible—when their damsons are in bloom.
But the land is wild, and there's a spirit of wildness
Much older, crying when the stone-curlew yodels
His sea and mountain cry, high up in Spring.
He nests in fields where still the gorse is free as
When all was open and common. Common 'tis named

And calls itself, because the bracken and gorse
Still hold the hedge where plough and scythe have
chased them.
Once on a time 'tis plain that the 'White Horse'
Stood merely on the border of a waste
Where horse or cart picked its own course afresh.
On all sides then, as now, paths ran to the inn;
And now a farm-track takes you from a gate.

Two roads cross, and not a house in sight
Except the 'White Horse' in this clump of beeches.
It hides from either road, a field's breadth back;
And it's the trees you see, and not the house,
Both near and far, when the clump's the highest thing
And homely too upon a far horizon
To one who knows there is an inn within. . . .

Edward Thomas

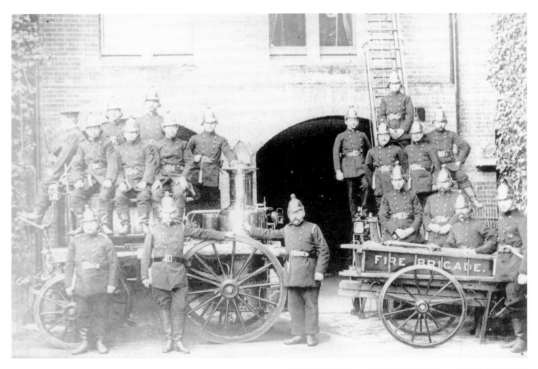

VOLUNTEER FIRE BRIGADE, WINCHESTER

FIRE

One autumn, after a long dry summer, when surrounding fields were reaped and threshing-engines, puffing and panting, were labouring at the ricks, a chance spark from one of these blown over the pretty roofs lodged in some sparrow's nest and crept among the rafters until it burst out with a yell of triumph. A brisk north-east wind brought me a puff of smoke, and I said: 'How foolish to burn brush on this windy day.' Then a woman came to tell me that it was no brush-burning but a house afire. With others I ran to the centre of the village where a row of connected cottages was already ablaze. The men in distant fields saw the flame and came hurrying home, but women were quick to release ponies and cows and drive them to safer enclosures—they had need to be quick to save anything. Presently all pails were filling and passing from hand to hand, but the wind mocked us, tossing balls of blazing straw across wide meadows, carrying the torch to stately trees, to dry hedges, and creeping into new thatches, filling the air with dark, horrible smoke. There was something particularly horrible in the voice of the fire. It roared with brutal triumph, pouring stinging smoke into our throats and eyes. Already the farmhouse nearest me seemed lost among its burning barns and stables. Fortunately it was tiled; that gave a little more time to save furniture. It was time to think of my own cottage. My maid and I put our clothing into boxes and carried them out together, fortunately with calmness enough to consider the direction of the wind, and make our heap of salvage away from it. People came to help, but I only accepted two whom I knew to be careful, and with their kind aid all my little treasures, even many of most fragile nature, were carried across the road to the middle of a field and protected by blankets. All this time the fire shouted and the smoke stung eyes and throats. All my furniture, except nailed-down carpets, was out, when, hurrah! on the top of the hill appears our hope, the fire-engine. After galloping five miles they had to descend the hill slowly, though every minute was impatient. In only half-an-hour from the outbreak of fire, one solid brick farmhouse with all its outbuildings, barns, and newly-gathered harvest was a crumbled mass of flame—a dozen dear little cottages were swept away, that great live oak opposite them still blazed as if in foliage of flame—and the fine barns and outhouses of another large farm were hopelessly involved. Now the engine got to work, and relays of eight men pumping together soon fixed the limit of destruction.

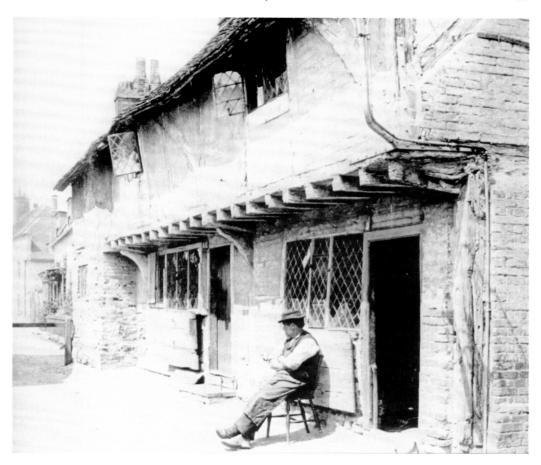

COTTAGE, ODIHAM

Then I went down the road, past ruins still steaming under streams of water, to the source of our disaster. Twelve pretty little houses, this morning gay in climbing roses, were shapeless heaps of ruin. In a pasture opposite, the poor inhabitants, in reckless haste and danger, had saved what they could, and now were trying, out of the confused salvage, to gather their own together and reckon their losses. All were homeless, dinnerless alike; prosperous people with a year's profits gone, old helpless people, poor labourers, with many children, were all suddenly dependent on their neighbours.

Anna Lea Merritt

THE WATCHERS

> By the ford at the town's edge
> Horse and carter rest:
> The carter smokes on the bridge
> Watching the water press in swathes about his horse's chest.
>
> From the inn one watches too,
> In the room for visitors
> That has no fire, but a view
> And many cases of stuffed fish, vermin, and kingfishers.

Edward Thomas

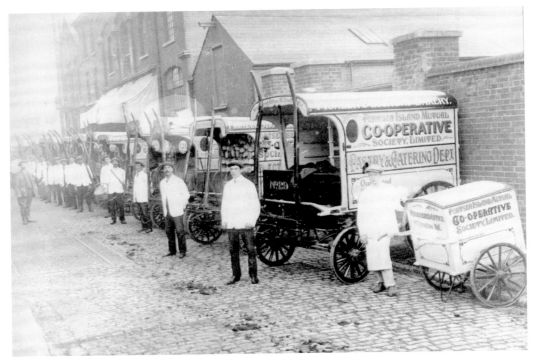

CO-OP VANS, PORTSEA ISLAND

SHOP ASSISTANT, BASINGSTOKE

I found on my arrival at the Co-op that I was not expected to serve in the shop right away, but was to have some time to get used to the variety of goods and the prices. During this period I worked in what was called 'Dispatch'. This was a room behind the shop in which orders were put up. In charge of this room was a little man with a fair moustache. He was not at all formidable as a 'boss', but was quiet and firm and slightly humorous and organized the work very well. The first job I was put to do was weighing sugar. Sacks of sugar were stored in a loft over Dispatch. This sugar was tipped down a shute to a bench below. It was my job to stand all day by this bench opening bags, filling sugar into them with a scoop and weighing them in one, two, three and four pounds. As a variation I sometimes switched over to lump sugar and when sufficient sugar had been done soda was sent down the shute. Soda was a commodity bought by most housewives before the advent of soap powders. After a few days at this rather monotonous task I was allowed to help with putting up orders. A very large number of these orders were from country customers. These were collected in late afternoon by the carriers who plied between villages and town.

Friday evening was a busy time in the shop, as many members came then to collect groceries and to pay bills. As bad luck would have it I was sent down for the first time to help on the grocery counter on a Friday evening. I was so bewildered that I am afraid I made a fine mess of things. I had to take payment of bills and the method of receipting had not been explained to me. When trying to serve customers I did not know where things were kept, nor yet had I memorized all the prices. I had not acquired the knack of making tidy packets for goods like dried fruit, rice and tapioca, and numerous others which were kept loose in drawers and had to be weighed as needed. To crown all, most customers expected their goods to be done up in a large paper parcel.

It seems now at this time, when all goods are packeted, and self-service is the order of the day, almost incredible the amount of work involved in serving just one customer under the old conditions. We sold some goods for which there was no room in the shop, such things as potatoes, corn for chickens, barley meal, bran and other animal feeding-stuffs which had to be measured in pint, quart or gallon measures and packed in paper bags. Another article was common salt, which came to the shop in long thick bars, from which we

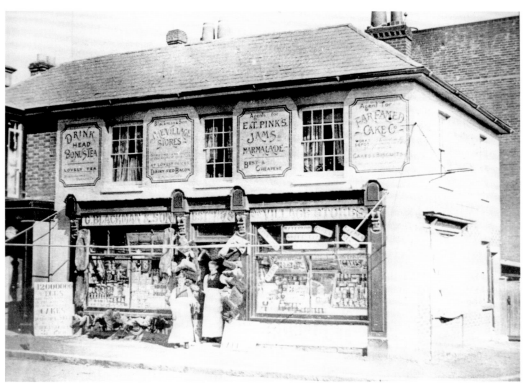

VILLAGE STORES, WATERLOOVILLE

had to cut a thick slice to be sold for 1½d. Yet another commodity was a long bar of household soap which might be bought whole or in halves or quarters and, for a change from solids, there was draught vinegar, to be drawn off into a measure and transferred to the customer's own bottle or jug. All these goods and others too were stored in rooms behind the shop and had to be fetched and weighed or measured as needed. The shop assistant's job was not a light one in those days, neither was it a clean one. So many things to weigh and so much to fetch and carry played havoc with our hands and with our overalls. We had a little retreat where we could wash our hands, in cold water, but too many trips to 'Scarborough', as it came to be called, were apt to be frowned upon. So we just wiped our hands on our overalls—and that was that! I soon learned to be wary of 'Committee men' who sometimes appeared without warning, and were suspected by the employees of 'snooping'. At the back of the grocery premises was a baker's where not only bread but confectionery was made. One of our shop windows was given over to a display of cakes which could be bought at the provision counter. In course of time I was given the job of dressing this window and I found it a pleasant interlude.

Winifred Griffiths

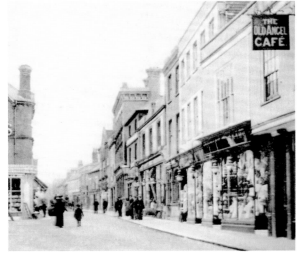

LONDON STREET, BASINGSTOKE

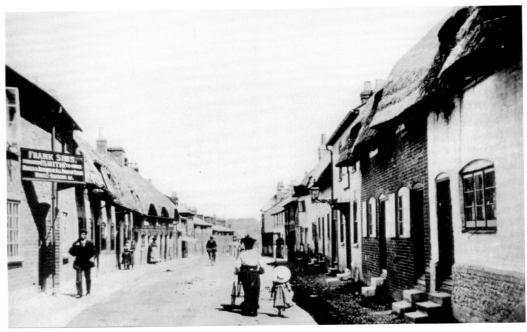

NEW STREET, ANDOVER

THE CARRIER

Fifty years ago the journey to the neighbouring market town of Andover could be made twice weekly by the carrier's cart, which once a week made the twelve-mile journey to Newbury also. The cart was hooded for wet weather, had fixed wooden benches and was drawn at little more than walking pace by one horse, the journey of five miles to Andover taking over an hour, with pauses on the way for the delivery of parcels or setting down of passengers. It went on Mondays and on Fridays—market day—and brought back from the outer world the local weekly newspaper, which gave information about what was happening in the villages around; reported every cricket match with scores and bowling; told the story of every Sunday School treat, with the names of the winning prizes; recorded births, marriages, with detailed descriptions, and deaths with obituary notices and lists of all at the funeral. Friday was a red-letter day because of its enlivening arrival, and each item of news was read, commented on and discussed.

The carrier's cart was regarded as so much a local institution that, when one day the news came round that his horse had dropped dead in the shafts on a journey, a collection was made in the village to help him to purchase a successor.

Kathleen E. Innes

QUEEN VICTORIA'S JUBILEE

The jubilee of our dear Queen we kept as well as we could. The hamlet dressed itself in flags and garlands. A procession was made in which everybody took part, dressed in costumes of the beginning of the reign. Mr Anthony headed it in an inherited smock-frock—a true old one, elaborately decorated with scrolls of stitching, a top-hat, and a huge nosegay of red and blue flowers. The blacksmith with a real anvil and forge, and other skilled mechanics, were drawn in a great waggon, festooned with flags and garlands. Superior citizens in strange costumes supposed to represent early Victorian days, were mounted on steeds caparisoned in patchwork counterpanes—and very elegant the horses looked! Suitable to the close of the century was a bevy of bicycle girls, with their wheels in garlands. The procession turned at the church, where it had great difficulty in carrying out the manoeuvre. The column fell into confusion for a time, but the knights on horseback galloped to and fro, and eventually led it safely to the favourite meadow, where a banquet was provided.

Anna Lea Merritt

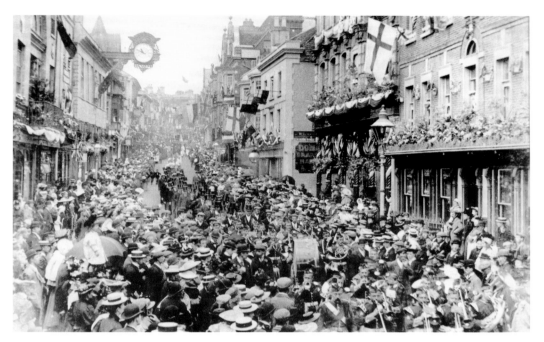

JUBILEE PROCESSION, WINCHESTER

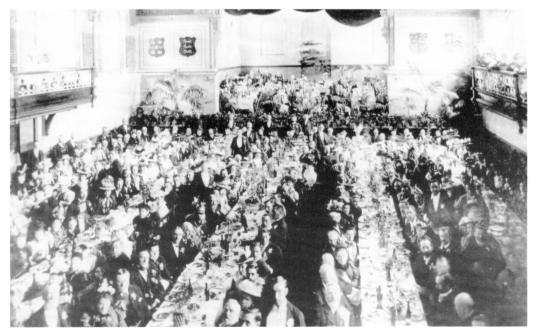

JUBILEE MEAL, WINCHESTER

THE HAVANT HORSE SHOW

The horse show annually organised by the Fareham and Hampshire Farmers' Club is indeed a progressive institution. Four years ago the first show was held in a small field at Fareham, and the insignificant sum of about £20 was taken at the gate. The show on Thursday occupied a great space on the green sward of Leigh Park, Havant, and altogether quite a gigantic affair. The show had all the elements of success about it. A warm sun

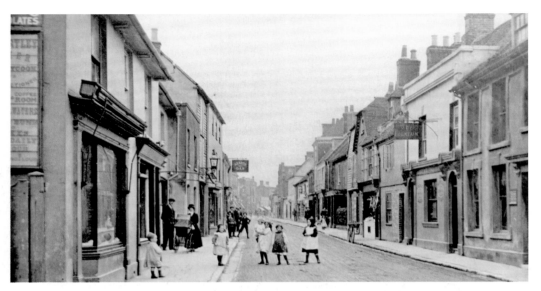

WEST STREET, HAVANT

smiled down on the grand old trees and stretches of green, and people went in crowds to witness the display of some of the best things in horseflesh in the county. The worthy people of Havant shut their shops at an early hour and repaired to the Park, and trainloads of spectators were brought to the town from all parts. To the ordinary spectator who just knows that a horse is an animal with four legs, one at each corner, there was the pure fresh air to breathe, with plenty of sights to interest. To those who know a good bit of horseflesh when they see it, the show was a perfect paradise. They revelled in the equine exhibits, discussed their good points, put on a horsey swagger, and were very important people. The members' enclosure was brilliant with crowds of pretty gowns, and the carriage enclosure and other places where all the sights could be seen for the humble shilling, were crowded.

ENTRIES AND PRIZES.

The prize list, subscriptions, and entries were nearly double those of last year, and there was also a substantial increase in the number of classes. About £230 was offered in prizes, and so keen was the competition, and of such excellent quality were the exhibits that the judges had a long and arduous task. The driving classes for ladies and gentlemen were the most popular, and so numerous were the entries that there were two classes each for ladies and gentlemen. The classes for cart horses, colts, geldings, and hunters were also well filled, and the tradesmen's turn-outs made a brave show with their sleek, well-kept horses and smart traps. In addition to the ordinary prizes several specials were offered. That well-known breeder, Sir Walter Gilby, gave a silver medal for the best foal of any age by a shire stallion. The brewers of Portsmouth also gave a champion prize for the best cart mare or gelding in the show.

The large staff of judges commenced their work at half-past ten, and they were kept hard at it until half-past six in the evening. The cart-horse classes came first, and some excellent cattle were shown.

PRIZE-WINNERS.

Most of the prizes were captured by Mr L. Deadman, of Brockhampton, Havant, his honours including seven firsts, three seconds, and two champion trophies—Sir Walter Gilby's medal for the best foal by a shire stallion, with 15-year-old roan mare descended from Harold, one of the best horses in England; and the prize presented by the brewers of Portsmouth and neighbourhood for the best cart mare, with his bay filly Blue Bell. Mr W. B. Martin, of Paulsgrove, Cosham, was also a very successful exhibitor, taking a first, a second, and a third prize for his cart mares, and a third for his yearling colt. Other prize-winners in those classes were Messrs F. Andrews, Barngreen; J. Bonham-Carter, Petersfield (two); J. Pink, Fareham; G. Wilder, Stansted Park, Emsworth (two); R. Hind, Petersfield (two); G. Brown, Horndean; W. Munday, Hambledon; G. Street, Hayling Island; R. Christie, Emsworth; J. Pope, Petersfield (two); and Miss Lyon, Emsworth (four).

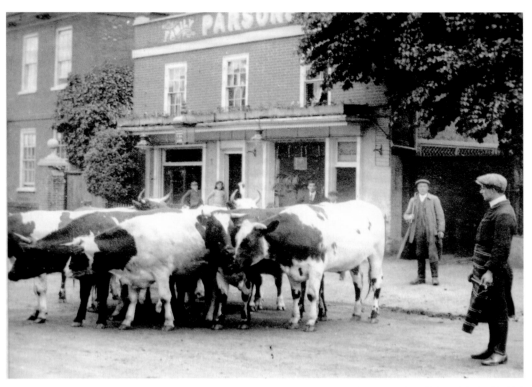

CATTLE IN THE STREET, ODIHAM

DRIVING CLASSES.

There was a particularly good show in these classes, the cattle being nearly all of first-class quality. Miss Lyon, of Emsworth, and Mrs R. C. Davis, Winchester, were awarded first prizes; Miss E. Greenwood, Droxford, and Mr G. Turner, Emsworth, seconds, and Mr A. Tennant, Petersfield, and Miss Clarke, Denmead, thirds. Mr H. P. L. Trescott, Chichester, Mr P. Lloyd, Admiralty House, Portsmouth, Dr J. MacGregor, St Mary's-crescent, Portsmouth, and Mr B. Thorpe, Emsworth, were also successful.

TRADESMEN'S LITTLE LOTS.

The classes for tradesmen were very interesting, the turnouts looking smart and bright with new paint and varnish. Messrs J. Budd, Eastleigh, C. Jackman, Albert-road, Southsea, and R. Batchelor, Landport, were successful butchers and Messrs Chatfield and Whettam, and Preston and Co. took honours among the Havant tradesmen.

THE 'MOKES.'

The donkeys turned up in full strength and romped over the course in gallant style, a trap-load of pretty, merry children—the little Misses Read, of Portchester, were easy winners of first honours.

HUNTERS.

It was in the hunters' classes that most of the interest centred. There was such a glorious uncertainty about the noble prancing steeds, you never knew whether they would suddenly go for the spectators, dash into the luncheon-tent, or waltz among the band. So numerous were the entries for the best hunter that the class had to be divided into two. After careful judging, winning rosettes were worn by Captain E. Adderley, Hambledon, the Hon. Mrs Baring, Meonstoke, Mr W. Dawtrey, Petworth, Mr G. S. Prior, Horndean, and Mr C. Daniels, Winchester. There were prizes offered for the best hunter suitable for carrying a lady, and many fine steeds there were, and many fine ladies, too. Dealing solely with the merits of the former, the judges gave the Hon. Mrs Barring first prize, Miss Scott, Shirley, second, and Miss Greenwood, Droxford, third.

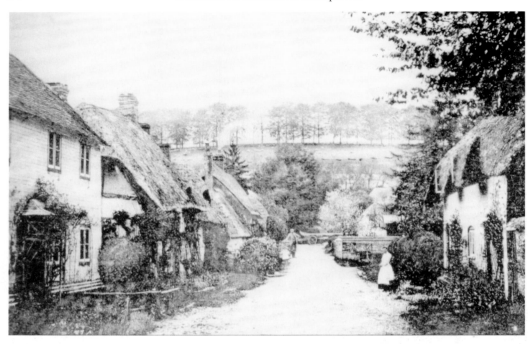

CHURCH STREET, WHERWELL

JUMPING.

As the finale of an excellent show, there was some splendid jumping by hunters. The competitors, for the most part, took the obstacles beautifully, although one or two came to grief at the water jump. The lady riders took the leaps in dashing style, one horsewoman managing her mount, who was filled with an overwhelming desire to turn back somersaults, in a very skilful way. Mr A. H. Shotter, Godalming, was the first-prize winner, Mr H. T. L. Triscott, Chichester, being second, and Mr T. Field, Chichester, third.

Lady FitzWygram presented the prizes.

Hampshire Telegraph

THE LANE

Some day, I think, there will be people enough
In Froxfield to pick all the blackberries
Out of the hedges of Green Lane, the straight
Broad lane where now September hides herself
In bracken and blackberry, harebell and dwarf gorse.
Today, where yesterday a hundred sheep
Were nibbling, halcyon bells shake to the sway
Of waters that no vessel ever sailed. . . .
It is a kind of spring: the chaffinch tries
His song. For heat it is like summer too.
This might be winter's quiet. While the glint
Of hollies dark in the swollen hedges lasts—
One mile—and those bells ring, little I know
Or heed if time be still the same, until
The lane ends and once more all is the same.

Edward Thomas

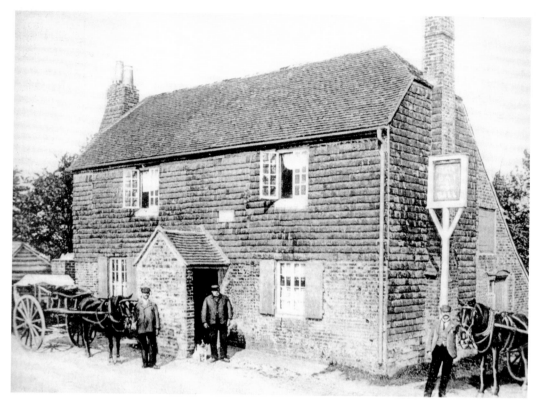

BAT AND BALL, HAMBLEDON

CRICKET

It is our pleasing duty to congratulate the Hampshire Cricket Club, as representing the County which was the original home of the national game, upon the advances it has made this season. There is a growing advocacy in influential quarters that Hampshire should be classed among the leading counties. Derbyshire made the recommendation the other day, and at a fully attended meeting of the Yorkshire County Committee on Wednesday, the same recommendation was also agreed upon. As the Derby correspondent of the *Athletic News* convincingly puts it:- 'Although Hampshire is reckoned a second-class county, they can unquestionably play cricket in first-class style. If anyone doubts this assertion let him apply to the cricketers of Essex, Derbyshire and Warwickshire, who within ten days have had to bite the dust before the South countrymen.'

Hampshire Telegraph, 18 August 1894

PORTSMOUTH MARKET

Carts and trucks increased by the score every moment. Soon the road way became blocked, narrowed as it was in one part by the drainage works and in all parts by the rows of carts and barrows and stalls on each side. It is very bad at the best of times, but on this occasion it was worse than usual. The stalls are not allowed on the pavements now, either, which narrows the roadway again. The trucks and carts filled up the space, and having been got alongside the waggons, a quick loading process went on. Greens, rhubarb, fruit, flowers, and all the hundred-and-one miscellaneous kinds of produce were bundled from the country waggons to the smaller vehicles, and the noise and movement grew ever more and more. And still the carts and trucks arrived. The police, a strong body of whom had come on duty at six o'clock, worked hard to keep the road clear, but, of course, failed. They backed the horses, pulled them forward, and turned the carts at right angles; they pushed trucks this way and that, shouted directions, and worked heroically. Thus, and thus only, could any movement be made. The loaded

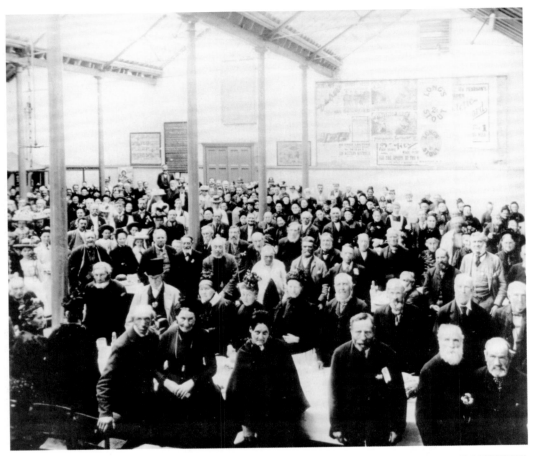

JUBILEE LUNCH, WINCHESTER

carts wanted to get out of and the empty ones to get into, the crowded, narrow way. By skilful management, and with numerous bumps and scratches and numberless collisions, some of the drivers did what they wanted to do, but it was trying work, and they had to wait so long. As time went on the babel grew worse, more carts arrived, and more got entangled and locked. At a quarter to seven a tram which conveys the postmen to North End started to get through from All Saints' Church. By shunting some of the vehicles into Oxford-street, and manipulating others with bewildering evolutions, the feat was accomplished, and the tram got clear after 21 minutes' purgatory. Then it had to go back! The confusion was distressing, and added to it was the bustle of the Dockyardmen going to work and of the stream of purchasers.

Our poor reporter got tired of it. He was butted in the back by carts about seventy times, hit in the ribs by trucks forty-one times, and nearly run over about eighty-three times. At eight o'clock he dodged and elbowed through the throng and went home. When he left, the road was still blocked, carts were entangled, and the police were pushing, pulling, piloting the loaded vehicles out. The pavements were crowded with buyers, and the air was full of shouts, clatter, and all the other indescribable noises incidental to a hurly-burly of the kind. The last sounds he heard as he got round a corner and wiped his brow were ''Eer's quollity for ya!' 'Fine oringe!' 'All a-blowin' and agrowin'!' and 'Mind where yer comin' with that bloomin' 'orse.'

Hampshire Telegraph, 11 May 1895

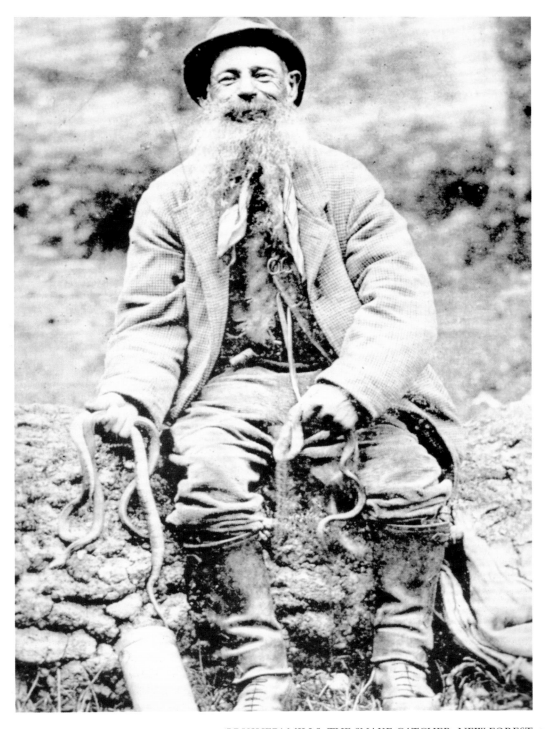

'BRUSHER' MILLS, THE SNAKE CATCHER, NEW FOREST

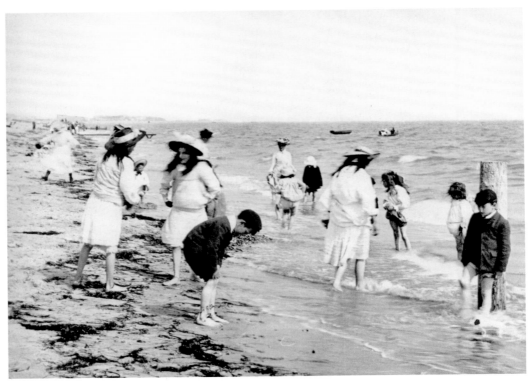

BEACH, HAYLING ISLAND

SEA BATHING

A discussion has been raised in the *Daily Graphic* as to the rival merits of home and foreign modes of sea-bathing. No one who had practised both can have any doubt as to the superior merits of the latter. In England a sea-bath may be healthy, but it is only available under the maximum of discomfort. Abroad, everything is done to render it pleasant. Why are the British sexes alone to be separated? Abroad, men and women, decently clothed, disport themselves in the water. Why not? A lady in a bathing-dress such as is worn in France is a far more decent object than a lady at a ball. I was once talking to an eminent Tory statesman. He told me that he had lately been to Paris with his wife, and, having nothing better to do, accompanied her to her dressmaker. 'She was having a bathing-dress made, and, would you believe it, she was insisting upon a lot of wadding being worked in to round her off where rounding seemed to be needed!'

Hampshire Telegraph, 31 August 1895

RELIGIOUS CUSTOMS

Twenty-five years ago, the labourers came to church in white gabardines and looked, at a little distance, like choirmen in surplices; only, the gabardine had elaborate gatherings and ornamental stitchings back and front, in the working of which it was, at one time, the pride of the good housewife to excel. One or two old men still wear the old garment, but among the younger it is seen no more; they have discarded it in favour of the cheap ready-made shoddy suit, with the dandy accompaniment of watch chain and brilliant-hued necktie. In like manner, the picturesque red cloaks, once the glory of all the elderly matrons, have, it is to be regretted, disappeared, with one exception, from the scene. The custom of the men sitting apart from the women in church, still prevails to some extent, but they congregate chiefly at the west end, while the women sit before them.

Some good old customs are dying out or neglected. The old people used to bow to the altar as they entered church and they were accustomed to make due and lowly reverence at the Name of the HOLY TRINITY, but the

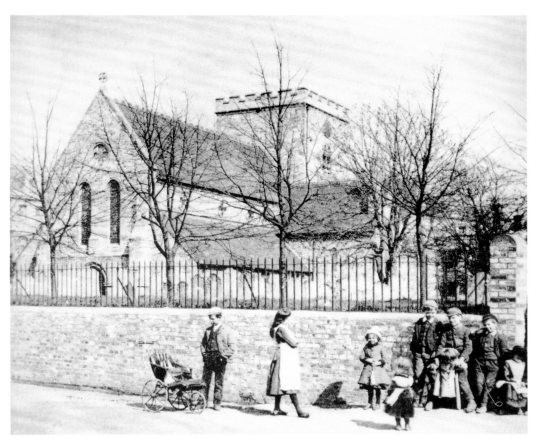

CHURCH, HAVANT

old people are gone and their children and grandchildren will not observe the ancient custom, though they have been repeatedly reminded of it from the pulpit. This neglect does not proceed from any dread of superstitious observances, but simply from a want of religious reverence. There is plenty of superstition left, but it is not religious superstition. The scepticism which is abroad in the world, finds its way even into the most secluded parishes. It is easy to see how—it is the result of continual change. Some of the cottages have changed their tenants several times, and on the whole, full three-fourths of the present inhabitants are new comers; no wonder then that old customs die out. What is worse, the new comers, as a rule, are not communicants, and the young people who have been confirmed have nearly all left the parish.

T. Hervey

HAMPSHIRE LANDSCAPE

Hampshire is, and always has been, a woodland county, and its forests have been much concerned with its history. Its natural features have had a great influence on the growth of its forests, for oak grows on the clay lands in all parts of the county, while beech flourishes on the loamy soils lying upon the slopes of the chalk hills, and upon similar soils in the north and south, and those areas which contain more sand than clay can be distinguished by a growth of pines and firs. Much of the land on the chalk hills was formerly old downland, a great part of which was the common pasture-land of the ancient manors until the time of the inclosures, since which time most of it has been broken up and cultivated in large fields, under the modern system of sheep farming.

T. W. Shore

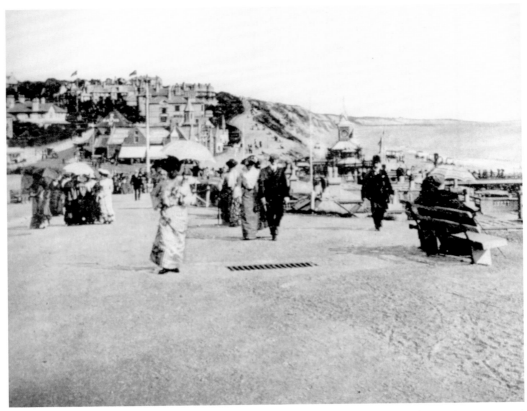

WEST CLIFF, BOURNEMOUTH

BOURNEMOUTH

In the south-west of Hampshire a great town is rapidly rising into importance. Half a century ago the Bourne was but the name of the beautiful little stream which now flows down the wooded vale into the sea, through the ornamental public grounds of Bournemouth. The town which has risen on both sides of this Bourne is already miles in extent in both directions. Its stately buildings, wooded drives, and its beach, which is scarcely surpassed by that of any other place, attract to it a never-ending stream of visitors, of which those in the winter are as important to its prosperity as those in the summer.

T. W. Shore

HAMPSHIRE PEOPLE

On going directly from any other district in southern England to the central parts of Hampshire one is sensible of a difference in the people. One is still in southern England, and the peasantry, like the atmosphere, climate, soil, the quiet but verdurous and varied scenery, are more or less like those in other neighbouring counties—Surrey, Sussex, Kent, Berkshire, Wilts, and Dorset. In general appearance, at all events, the people are much the same; and the dialect, where any survives, and even the quality of the voices, closely resemble those in adjoining counties. Nevertheless there is a difference; even the hasty seers who are almost without the faculty of observation are vaguely cognisant of it, though they would not be able to say what it consisted in. Probably it would puzzle any one to say wherein Hampshire differed from all the counties named, since each has something individual. They would probably say that the people of Hampshire were less good-looking, that they had less red colour in their skins, less pure colour in their eyes; they had less energy, if not less intelligence, or at all events were less lively, and had less humour.

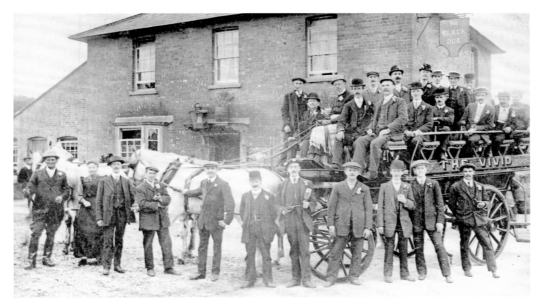

RAILWAY WORKERS, EASTLEIGH

The majority of the people are divisible into four fairly distinct types, the minority being composed of intermediate forms and nondescripts. There is an enormous disproportion in the actual numbers of the people of these distinct types, and it varies greatly in different parts of the county. Of the Hampshire people it may be said generally, as we say of the whole nation, that there are two types—the blonde and the dark; but in this part of England there are districts where a larger proportion of dark blood than is common in England generally has produced a well-marked intermediate type; and this is one of my four distinct Hampshire types. I should place it second in importance, although it comes a very long way after the first type, which is distinctly blonde.

This first most prevalent type, which greatly outnumbers all the others put together, and probably includes more than half of the entire population, is strongest in the north, and extends across the county from Sussex to Wiltshire. The Hampshire people in that district are hardly to be distinguished from those of Berkshire. One can see this best by looking at the schoolchildren in a number of North Hampshire and Berkshire villages. In sixty or seventy to a hundred and fifty children in a village school you will seldom find as many as a dozen with dark eyes.

There is very little beauty or good looks in this people; on the other hand, there is just as little downright ugliness; they are mostly on a rather monotonous level, just passable in form and features, but with an almost entire absence of any brightness, physical or mental. Take the best looking woman of this most common type—the description will fit a dozen in any village. She is of medium height, and has a slightly oval face (which, being Anglo-Saxon, she ought not to have), with fairly good features; a nose fairly straight, or slightly thin; chin frequently pointed. Her hair is invariably brown, without any red or chestnut colour in it, generally of a dull or dusty hue; and the eyes are a pale greyish-blue, with small pupils, and in very many cases a dark mark round the iris. The deep blue, any pure blue, in fact, from forget-me-not to ultramarine, is as rare in this commonest type as warm or bright hair—chestnut, red or gold; or as a brilliant skin. The skin is pallid, or dusky, or dirty looking. Even healthy girls in their teens seldom have any colour, and the exquisite roseate and carmine reds of other counties are rare indeed. The best looking girls at the time of life when they come nearest to being pretty, when they are just growing into womanhood, have an unfinished look which is almost pathetic. One gets the fancy that Nature had meant to make them nice-looking, and finally becoming dissatisfied with her work, left them to grow to maturity anyhow. It is pathetic, because there was little more to be done—a rosier blush on the cheek, a touch of scarlet on the lips, a little brightness and elasticity in the hair, a pencil of sunlight to make the eyes sparkle.

In figure this woman is slim, too narrow across the hips, too flat in the chest. And she grows thinner with years. The number of lean, pale women of this type in Hampshire is very remarkable. You see them in every village,

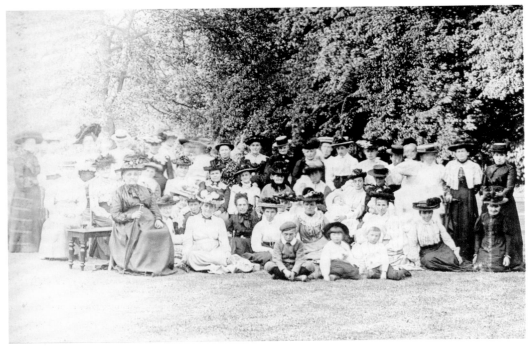

MOTHERS' UNION, EVERSLEY

women that appear almost fleshless, with a parchment-like skin drawn tight over the bones of the face, pale-blue, washed-out eyes, and thin, dead-looking hair. What is the reason of this leanness? It may be that the women of this blond type are more subject to poverty of blood than others; for the men, though often thin, are not so excessively thin as the women. Or it may be the effect of that kind of poison which cottage women all over the country are becoming increasingly fond of, and which is having so deleterious an effect on the people in many counties—the tea they drink. Poison it certainly is: two or three cups a day of the black juice which they obtain by boiling and brewing the coarse Indian teas at a shilling a pound which they use, would kill me in less than a week.

Or it may be partly the poison of tea and partly the bad conditions, especially the want of proper food, in the villages. One day on the downs near Winchester I found a shepherd with his flock, a man of about fifty, and as healthy and strong looking a fellow as I have seen in Hampshire. Why was it, I asked him, that he was the only man of his village I had seen with the colour of red blood in his face? why did they look so unwholesome generally? why were the women so thin, and the children so stunted and colourless? He said he didn't know, but thought that for one thing they did not get enough to eat. 'On the farm where I work,' he said, 'there are twelve of us—nine men, all married, and three boys. My wages are thirteen shillings, with a cottage and garden; I have no children, and I neither drink nor smoke, and have not done so for eighteen years. Yet I find the money is not too much. Of the others, the eight married men all have children—one has got six at home: they all smoke, and all make a practice of spending at least two evenings each week at the public house: How, after paying for beer and tobacco, they could support their families on the few shillings that remained out of their wages was a puzzle to him.

But this is to digress. The prevalent blond type I have tried to describe is best seen in the northern half of the county, but is not so accentuated on the east, north, and west borders as in the interior villages. If, as is commonly said, this people is Anglo-Saxon, it must at some early period have mixed its blood with that of a distinctly different race. This may have been the Belgic or Brythonic, but as shape and face are neither Celtic nor Saxon, the Brythons must have already been greatly modified by some older and different race which they, or the Goidels before them, had conquered and absorbed. It will be necessary to return to this point by-and-by.

Side by side with this, in a sense, dim and doubtful people, you find the unmistakable Saxon, the thick set, heavy looking, round-headed man with blue eyes and light hair and heavy drooping mustacios—a sort of terrestrial

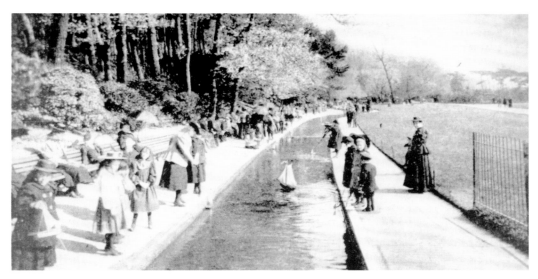

CENTRAL GARDENS, BOURNEMOUTH

walrus who goes erect. He is not abundant as in Sussex, but is represented in almost any village, and in these villages he is always like a bulldog or bull terrier among hounds, lurchers, and many other varieties, including curs of low degree. Mentally, he is rather a dull dog, at all events deficient in the finer, more attractive qualities. Leaving aside the spiritual part, he is a good all round man, tough and stubborn, one the naturalist may have no secret qualms about in treating as an animal. A being of strong animal nature, and too often in this brewer-ridden county a hard drinker. A very large proportion of the men in rural towns and villages with blotchy skins and water or beery eyes are of this type. Even more offensive than the animality, the mindlessness, is that flicker of conscious superiority which lives in their expression. It is, I fancy, a survival of the old instinctive feeling of a conquering race amid the conquered.

Nature, we know, is everlastingly harking back, but here in Hampshire I cannot but think that this type, in spite of its very marked character, is a very much muddied and degenerate form. One is led to this conclusion by occasionally meeting with an individual whose whole appearance is a revelation, and strikes the mind with a kind of astonishment, and one can only exclaim—there is nothing else to say—Here Nature has at length succeeded in reproducing the pure unadulterated form! Such a type I came upon one summer day on the high downs east of the Itchen.

He was a shepherd, a young fellow of twenty, about five feet eight in height, but looking short on account of his extraordinary breadth of shoulders and depth of chest. His arms were like a blacksmith's, and his legs thick, and his big head was round as a Dutch cheese. He could, I imagined, have made a breach in the stone wall near which I found him with his flock, if he had lowered that hard round

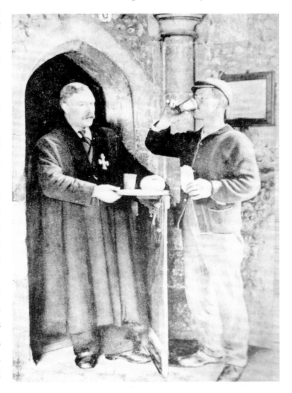

ST CROSS DOLE, WINCHESTER

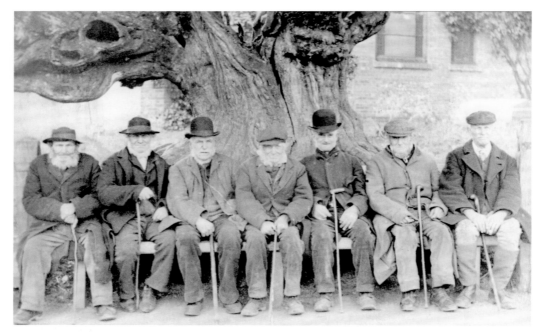

VILLAGE ELDERS, FAIR OAK

head and charged it like a rhinocerous. His hair was light brown, and his face a uniform rosy brown—in all Hampshire no man or woman had I seen so beautiful in colour, and his round, keen, piercing eyes were of a wonderful blue—'eyes like the sea'. If this poor fellow, washed clean and clothed becomingly in white flannels, had shown himself in some great gathering at the Oval or some such place on some great day, the common people would have parted on either side to make way for him, and would have regarded him with a kind of worship—an impulse to kneel before him. There, on the downs, his appearance was almost grotesque in the dress he wore, made of some fabric intended to last for ever, but now frayed, worn to threads in places, and generally earth coloured. A small old cap, earth-coloured too, covered a portion of his big, round head, and his ancient, lumpish, cracked and clouted boots were like the hoofs of some extinct large sort of horse which he had found fossilised among the chalk hills. He had but eleven shillings a week, and could not afford to spend much on dress. How he could get enough to eat was a puzzle; he looked as if he could devour half of one of his muttons at a meal, washed down with a bucket of beer, without hurt to his digestion. In appearance he formed a startling contrast to the people around him: they were in comparison a worn-out, weary looking race, dim eyed, pale faced, slow in their movements, as if they had lost all joy and interest in life.

The sight of him taught me something I could not get from the books. The intensity of life in his eyes and whole expression: the rough hewn face and rude, powerful form—rude but well balanced—the vigour in his every movement, enabled me to realize better than anything that history tells us what those men who came as strangers to these shores in the fifth century were really like, and how they could do what they did. They came, a few at a time, in open row boats, with nothing but their rude weapons in their hands, and by pure muscular force, and because they were absolutely without fear and without compassion, and were mentally but little above a herd of buffaloes, they succeeded in conquering a great and populous country with centuries of civilization behind it.

This, then, is one of the main facts to be noted in the blonde Hampshire peasant—the great contrast between the small minority of persons of the Anglo-Saxon and of the prevalent type. It was long ago shown by Huxley that the English people generally are not Saxons in the shape of the head, and in all Saxon England the divergence has perhaps been greatest in this southern county. The oval-faced type, as I have said, is less pronounced as we approach the borders of Berkshire, and although the difference is not very great, it is quite perceptible; the Berkshire people are rather nearer to the common modified Saxon type of Oxfordshire and the Midlands generally.

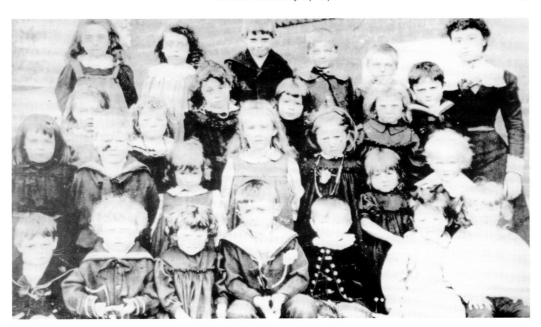

CHILDREN, NETLEY

In the southern half of Hampshire the dark-eyed, black-haired people are almost as common as the blonde, and in some localities they are actually in a majority. Visitors to the New Forest district often express astonishment at the darkness and 'foreign' appearance of the people, and they sometimes form the mistaken idea that it is due to a strong element of gipsy blood. The darkest Hampshire peasant is always in shape of head and face the farthest removed from the gipsy type.

Among the dark people there are two distinct types, as there are two in the blonde, and it will be understood that I only mean two that are, in a measure, fixed and easily recognized types; for it must always be borne in mind that, outside of these distinctive forms, there is a heterogeneous crowd of persons of all shades and shapes of face and of great variety in features. These two dark types are—first, the small, narrow-headed person of brown skin, crow-black hair, and black eyes; of this rarest and most interesting type I shall speak last. Second, the person of average height, slightly oval face, and dark eyes and hair. Now we find that this dark-haired, dark-eyed, and often dark-skinned people are in stature, figure, shape of head, and features exactly like the oval-faced blonde people already described. They are, light and dark, an intermediate type, and we can only say that they are one and the same people, the outcome of a long mixed race which has crystallized in this form unlike any of its originals; that the difference in colour is due to the fact that blue and black in the iris and black and brown in the hair very seldom mix, these colours being, as has been said, 'mutually exclusive'. They persist when everything else, down to the bony framework, has been modified and the original racial characters obliterated. Nevertheless, we see that these mutually exclusive colours do mix in some individuals both in the eyes and hair. In the grey-blue iris it appears as a very slight pigmentation, in most cases round the pupil, but in the hair it is more marked. Many, perhaps a majority, of the dark-eyed people we are now considering have some warm brown colour in their black hair; in members of the same family you will often find raven-black hair and brownish-black hair; and sometimes in three brothers or sisters you will find the two original colours, black and brown, and the intermediate very dark or brownish-black hair.

The brunette of this oval-faced type is also, as we have seen, deficient in colour, but, as a rule, she is more attractive than her light-eyed sister. This may be due to the appearance of a greater intensity of life in the dark eye; but it is also probable that there is almost always some difference in disposition, that black or dark pigment is correlated with a warmer, quicker, more sympathetic nature. The anthropologists tell us that very slight differences in intensity of pigmentation may correspond to relatively very great constitutional differences. One fact in reference to dark- and light-coloured people which I came upon in Hampshire struck me as exceedingly curious, and has suggested

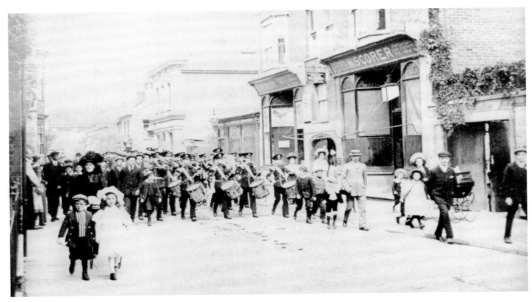

NORTH STREET, HAVANT

the question: Is there in us, or in some of us, very deep down, and buried out of sight, but still occasionally coming to life and to the surface, an ancient feeling of repulsion or racial antipathy between black and blonde?

Here in Hampshire I have been startled at some things I have heard spoken by dark-eyed people about blondes. Not of the mitigated Hampshire blonde, with that dimness in the colour of his skin, and eyes, and hair, but of the more vivid type with brighter blue eyes, and brighter or more fiery hair, and the light skin to match. What I have heard was to this effect:

'Perhaps it will be all right in the end—we hope it will: he says he will marry her and give her a home. But you never know where you are with a man of that colour—I'll believe it when I see it.'

'Yes, he seems all right, and speaks well, and promises to pay me the money. But look at the colour of his eyes! No, I can't trust him.'

'He's a very nice person, I have no doubt, but his eyes and hair are enough for me.' &c., &c.

Even this may be merely the effect of that enmity or suspicion with which the stranger, or 'foreigner', as he is called, is often regarded in rural districts. The person from another county, or from a distance, unrelated to any one in the community, is always a foreigner, and the foreign taint may descend to the children: may it not be that in Hampshire any one with bright colour in eyes, hair, and skin is also by association regarded as a foreigner?

It remains to speak of the last of the four distinct types, the least common and most interesting of all—the small, narrow-headed man with very black hair, black eyes, and brown skin.

We are deeply indebted to the anthropologists who have, so to speak, torn up the books of History, and are re-telling the story of Man on earth: we admire them for their patient industry, and because they have gone bravely on with their self-appointed task, one peculiarly difficult in this land of many mixed races, heedless of the scoffs of the learned or of those who derive their learning from books alone, and mock at men whose documents are 'bones and skins'. But we sometimes see that they (the anthropologists) have not yet wholly emancipated themselves from the old written falsehoods when they tell us, as they frequently do, that the Iberian in this country survives only in the west and the north. They refer to the small, swarthy Welshman; to the so-called 'black Celt' in Ireland, west of the Shannon; to the small black Yorkshireman of the Dales, and to the small black Highlander; and the explanation is that in these localities remnants of the dark men of the Iberian race who inhabited Britain in the Neolithic period, were never absorbed by the conquerors; that, in fact, like the small existing herds of indigenous -white cattle, they have preserved their peculiar physical character down to the present time by remaining unmixed with the Surrounding blue-eyed people. But this type is not confined to these isolated spots in the west and north;

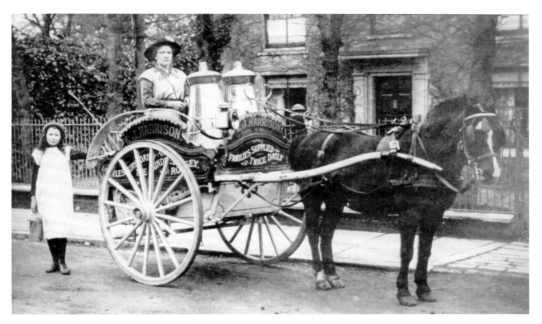

MILK CART, ROMSEY

it is found here, there, and everywhere, especially in the southern counties of England: you cannot go about among the peasants of Hampshire, Wiltshire, and Dorset without meeting examples of it, and here, at all events, it cannot be said that the ancient British people were not absorbed. They, the remnant that escaped extermination, were absorbed by the blue-eyed, broad-headed, tall men, the Goidels we suppose, who occupied the country at the beginning of the Bronze Age; and the absorbers were in their turn absorbed by another blue-eyed race; and these by still another or by others. The only explanation appears to be that this type is persistent beyond all others, and that a very little black blood, after being mixed and re-mixed with blonde for centuries, even for hundreds of generations, may, whenever the right conditions occur, reproduce the vanished type in its original form.

In speaking of the character, physical and mental, of the men of distinctly Iberian type, I must confess that I write only from my own observation, and that I am hardly justified in founding general statements on an acquaintance with a very limited number of persons. My experience is that the men of this type have, generally speaking, more character than their neighbours, and are certainly very much more interesting. In recalling individuals of the peasant class who have most attracted me, with whom I have become intimate and in some instances formed lasting friendships, I find that of twenty-five to thirty no fewer than nine are of this type. Of this number four are natives of Hampshire, while the other five, oddly enough, belong to five different counties. But I do not judge only from these few individuals: a rambler about the country who seldom stays many days in one village or spot cannot become intimately acquainted with the cottagers. I judge partly from the few I know well, and partly from a very much larger number of individuals I have met casually or have known slightly. What I am certain of is that the men of this type, as a rule, differ mentally as widely as they do physically from persons of other commoner types. The Iberian, as I know him in southern and south western England, is, as I have said, more intelligent, or at all events, quicker; his brains are nimbler although perhaps not so retentive or so practical as the slower Saxon's. Apart from that point, he has more imagination, detachment, sympathy—the qualities which attract and make you glad to know a man and to form a friendship with him in whatever class he may be. Why is it, one is sometimes asked, that one can often know and talk with a Spaniard or Frenchman without any feeling of class distinction, any consciousness of a barrier, although the man may be nothing but a workman, while with English peasants this freedom and ease between man and man is impossible? It *is* possible in the case of the man we are considering simply because of those qualities I have named, which he shared with those of his own race on the continent.

W. H. Hudson

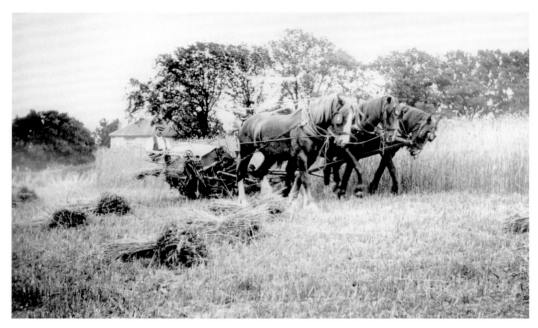

REAPING

THE REAPER

The oats have been trampled by rain, and two men are reaping it by hand. They are not men of the farm, but rovers who take their chance and have done other things than reaping in their time. One is a Hampshire man. . . of heroic build; tall, lean, rather deep-chested than broad-shouldered, narrow in the loins, with goodly calves which his old riding breeches perfectly display; his head is small, his hair short and crisp and fair, his cheeks and neck darkly tanned, his eye bright blue and quick-moving, his features strong and good, except his mouth, which is over large and loose; very ready to talk, which he does continually in a great proud male voice, however hard he is working. A man as lean and hard and bright as his reaping hook. First he snicks off a dozen straws and lays them on the ground for a bond, then he slashes fast along the edge of the corn for two or three yards, gathers up what is cut into his hook and lays it across the straws: when a dozen sheaves are prepared in the same way he binds them with the bonds and builds them into a stook of two rows leaning together. It is impossible to work faster and harder than he does in cutting and binding; only at the end of each dozen sheaves does he stand at his full height, straight as an ash, and laugh, and round off what he has been saying even more vigorously than he began it. Then crouching again he slays twelve other sheaves.

Edward Thomas

THE NEW FOREST

Between the Boldre and the Exe, or Beaulieu river, there is a stretch of country in most part flat and featureless. It is one of those parts of the Forest which have a bare and desolate aspect; here in places you can go a mile and not find a tree or bush, where nothing grows but a starved-looking heath, scarcely ankle-deep. Wild life in such places is represented by a few meadow pipits and small lizards. There is no doubt that this barrenness and naked appearance is the result of the perpetual cutting of heath and gorse, and the removal of the thin surface soil for fuel.

Beyond that starved, melancholy wilderness one comes to a point which overlooks the valley of the Exe; and here one pauses long before going down to the half-hidden village by the river. Especially if it is in May or June, when the oak is in its 'glad light grene', for that is the most vivid and beautiful of all vegetable greens, and the prospect is the greenest and most soul-refreshing to be found in England. The valley is all wooded and the wood is all oak—a continuous oak-wood stretching away on the right, mile on mile, to the sea. The sensation experienced

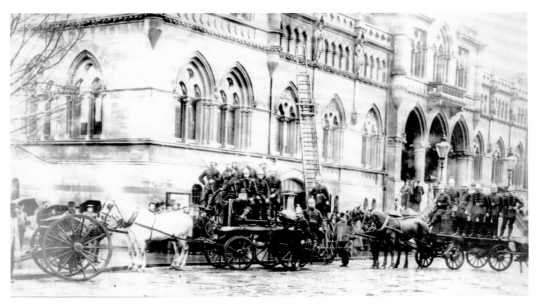

FIRE BRIGADE, WINCHESTER

at the sight of this prospect is like that of the traveller in a dry desert when he comes to a clear running stream and drinks his fill of water and is refreshed. The river is tidal, and at the full of the tide in its widest part beside the village its appearance is of a small inland lake.

W. H. Hudson

STEAM FIRE ENGINE

The new steam fire-engine purchased by the Local Board arrived in Fareham on Wednesday, and was on Thursday subjected to a series of trials by the members of the Fire Brigade. The engine, which was supplied by Messrs Shand, Mason, and Co., is known as the 'A Volunteer,' and is especially constructed for the use of Volunteer Brigades. In the absence of the Chairman of the Local Board (Captain Ramsay) the efficiency of the Brigade was demonstrated, and the engine was found to work in a satisfactory manner. In the evening the firemen paraded the town, led by the band of the 15th Company S.D. Royal Artillery, and were afterwards entertained at dinner at the Royal Oak by Mr A. Suston, the newly-appointed Captain of the Brigade.

Hampshire Telegraph, 13 October 1894

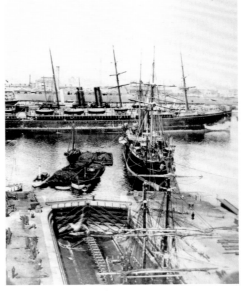

THE SEA
The sun set, the wind fell, the sea
Was like a mirror shaking:
The one small wave that clapped the land
A mile-long snake of foam was making
Where tide had smoothed and wind had dried
The vacant sand.

Edward Thomas

DOCKS, SOUTHAMPTON

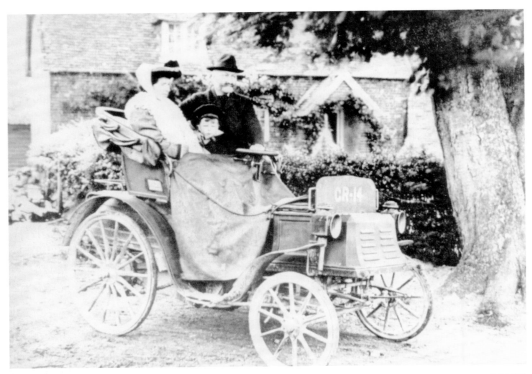

EARLY CAR, BISHOPSTOKE

A STEAM CAR

An important test case with respect to the designation of the newly-invented auto-car was heard at the Fareham Sessions, on Monday, before Mr W. H. Deane (Chairman) and other Magistrates.

John Adolphus Koosen, of 1, Sussex-place, Southsea, was summoned for using a locomotive on the Gosport-road, on the 9th inst., without causing a person on foot to precede it by at least twenty yards.

Mr Hobbs (Hyde and Hobbs) appeared for the defence.

Constable Kerby stated that he saw the autocar passing along the highway at a pace of from six to seven miles an hour. Steam was coming from the vehicle, in which the defendant and a lady were seated.

Mr Hobbs argued that the auto-car was a carriage, and not a locomotive, the license obtained from the Excise stating that it could be propelled or drawn by horses or mechanical power.

The Chairman: But it might be made a locomotive at any moment as a gig or any other vehicle might be attached at will.

Mr Hobbs said that might be so, but at present they had not done that. He further pointed out that if a conviction ensued it would greatly interfere with a growing industry, and would entail the obtaining of a special Act of Parliament, as autocars were now greatly used in Paris, America, and various English towns.

Mr J. R. Penning, electrician, Elm-grove, Southsea, proved that the autocar had four rubber tyred wheels, was like an ordinary elegant Victoria, with a perfect steering gear, able to stop within about seven feet, ejected but a small amount of hot water and vapour, and could do no possible harm to the roads.

Constable Kerby, recalled, repeated his assertion that steam was coming from the auto-car when he saw it at Stubbington.

Mr George Hackett, of Ryde, having seen the machine, said that no steam was emitted.

The Magistrates said they were unanimously of opinion that the carriage was a locomotive. Inasmuch as this was the first case of the kind, they imposed only a nominal penalty of 1s. and 15s. 7d. costs.

Hampshire Telegraph, 21 December 1895

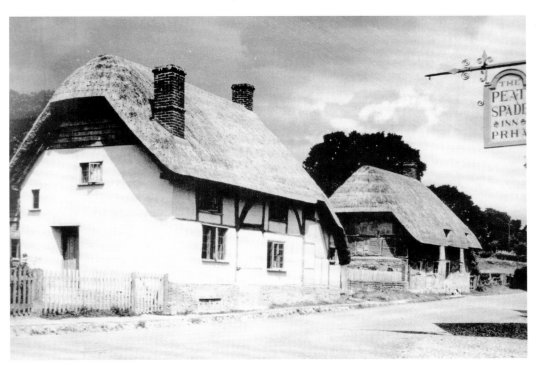

COTTAGE, LONGSTOCK

THE VILLAGE

Suddenly there is a village of thatched roofs, phlox in the gardens, good spaces of green and of sycamore-trees between one house and the next, and a green-weeded crystal river pervading all with its flash and sound. The anvil rings and the fire glows in the black smithy. The wheel-wright's timber leans outside his thatched shed against an ancient elder, etherealized by lucent yellow leaves. Before the inn a jolly ostler with bow legs and purple neck washes the wheels of a cart, ever and anon filling his pail from the stream and swishing the bright water over the wheels as they spin. A decent white-haired old man stands and watches, leaning on his stick held almost at arm's length so as to make an archway underneath which a spaniel sprawls in the sun. The men are all at the corn and he does not know what to do. Can he read? asks the ostler, knowing the answer very well. No! We all read now, chuckles the ostler as he flings a pailful over the wheel. The old man is proud at least to have lived into such a notable day: 'Yes, man reads now almost as well as master—quite as well. They used to be dummies, the working class people, yes, that they was. You can't tell what will happen now' Meantime the ostler fills his pail and the old man having too many thoughts to say any more, lays his blackthorn on the bench and calls for his glass of fourpenny ale.

Edward Thomas

WOODMAN'S COTTAGE

But the woodman's cot
By the ivied trees
Awakens not
To light or breeze.

It smokes aloft
Unwavering:
It hunches soft
Under storm's wing.

Edward Thomas

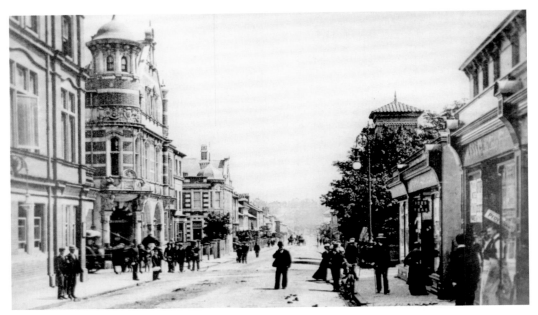

VICTORIA ROAD, ALDERSHOT

ALDERSHOT

The modern necessity for an improved military training of the army has been the cause of the growth of a considerable town in the east of the county, where Aldershot has risen from the condition of an insignificant village, and has become the chief training place for the army.

T. W. Shore

MAY DAY CUSTOMS

May Day is sometimes all that is lovely and genial, when the children and their flowers are all that their ideal should be. Cold east wind does not matter so much to them, but showers make their rounds dismal work. The custom varies a good deal, according as it has been fostered. Once boys in Devonshire were licensed to drench with water from cows' horns whoever did not wear a spray of maythorn. I can just remember a lady corning in, indignant and dripping.

In many towns there is a Jack-in-the-Green, attended by a rabble rout; in many villages, chiefly in the northern counties, a doll in the centre of an arbour of flowers is carried round and exhibited in return for halfpence, probably being a remnant of honour to an image of the Blessed Virgin on the opening of the month of Mary. In the south, however, it has often dwindled to small children wandering about with an untidy bunch of king-cups and cuckoo flowers at the end of a stick, quavering shrilly out—

> April's gone,
> May's come,
> Come and see our *garland*;

and halfpence being thrown out till the stock of them and of patience was exhausted, and the whole affair discouraged.

We have found the best way in our parts to be to sanction the whole school going together under some efficient guardian with one general money-box, the proceeds of which, when divided, have always proved more satisfactory than those of individual effort; or, at one parish, all is spent in a general tea, which, of course, gives delight.

We also make a May Queen, not the fairest maiden, as in song, but the youngest girl in the infant school, who appears in a white dress kept for the occasion, flower-wreathed, as well as her hat.

Charlotte M. Yonge

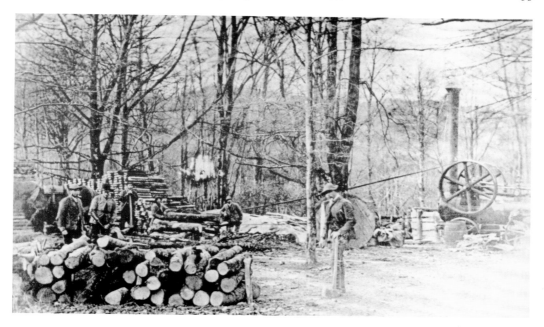

TIMBER WORKING, NEAR ALTON

A RAINY SUMMER ON HAYLING ISLAND

'I had been in prison on our island for many sad and desolate days. Not a vestige of blue sky by day, or a golden star by night. . . . The Isle of Wight was completely blotted out. Spithead and its forts were in tears. The Warner light could not flash through the grey gloom, and after dinner, pacing the conservatory of the "Bungalow Yacht", it was impossible for three long imprisoned evenings to see the welcome illumination on Southsea Pier. Our only consolation was to be told that the island wanted the rain very badly. Well, the island had got enough of it now, in all conscience. . . . After the rain the mushrooms appear to have had a gay time of it . . . and, from all accounts, the mushroom crop on our salt sea common will be able to dispute authority with the potsherds, broken bottles, and lost golf balls of which we invariably have a very plentiful harvest. For this is all that excursionists do on our deserted island. They come in wagons to have cock-shies at bottles of every shape and size, in order to torture, madden, and lacerate the bathers from the beach; and they lose golf balls by the dozen among the shingle and blackberry-bushes, to the huge satisfaction of the lynx-eyed "caddies", who get paid handsomely for lost balls when recovered.

Clement Scott

THE LABOURER

''Twill take some getting.' 'Sir, I think 'twill so:
The old man stared up at the mistletoe
That hung too high in the poplar's crest for plunder
Of any climber, though not for kissing under:
Then he went on against the north-east wind—
Straight but lame, leaning on a staff new-skinned,
Carrying a brolly, flag-basket, and old coat,—
Towards Alton, ten miles off: And he had not
Done less from Chilgrove where he pulled up docks.
'Twere best, if he had had 'a money-box',
To have waited there till the sheep cleared a field

For what a half-week's flint-picking would yield.
His mind was running on the work he had done
Since he left Christchurch in the New Forest, one
Spring in the 'seventies,—navvying on dock and line
From Southampton to Newcastle-on-Tyne, -
In 'seventy-four a year of soldiering
With the Berkshires,—hoeing and harvesting
In half the shires where corn and couch will grow.
His sons, three sons, were fighting, but the hoe
And reap-hook he liked, or anything to do with trees.

Edward Thomas

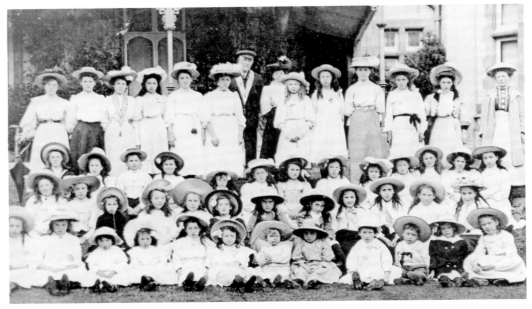

CHILDREN, BISHOPSTOKE

PRE-CHRISTMAS TRADITIONS

St Thomas's Day ushers in Christmas. In some Hampshire villages, St Thomas's Day is spent by all the poorer women in what they call 'gooding'—going from house to house to receive something towards the Christmas dinner. A shilling to each widow, and sixpence to each wife, is the traditional amount; but hardly any one keeps up the dole, since modern changes have come in, and neither squires, farmers, nor peasants are in the old semi-feudal connection. In most places some other form of Christmas gift has been substituted.

Another ordinance of St Thomas's Feast was the arrival of certain musical gipsies. 'It's the Lees!' has been the

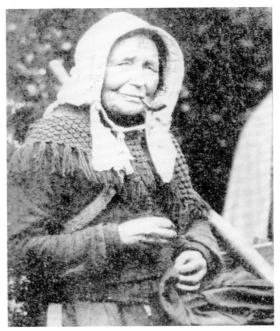

GYPSY QUEEN, NEW FOREST

answer when asking the cause of all outbreak of drumming and the like; but this likewise has nearly come to an end, and the genuine gipsy is not a very frequent creature. Moreover, he travels no longer in a picturesque, ramshackle tilted cart, where the red-kerchiefed mother and bright-eyed, brown-faced children look out as from a bower, but in a yellow van, with a stove-pipe protruding from it. And he often has quarters in a town for the winter.

One genuine family was here some years ago, of thorough gipsy blood. A woman was very ill, and a kind gentleman let them remain in his field and sent broth and wine. They were strictly honest, and even refused offers of help from other quarters, saying that they were fully provided for. The woman died, and they lamented her with loud cries like Easterns. They talked of putting up a stone to her, but have never done so. Her name was Gerania.

This gipsy music is not connected with carols. Those carols, in the old time, had a flavour of wild beauty about them. I remember standing in the

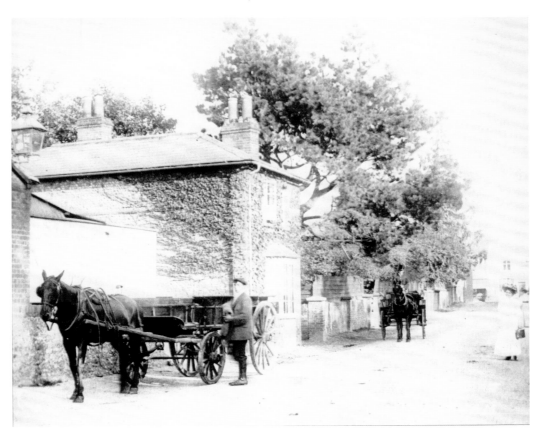

STATION ROAD, BISHOP'S WALTHAM

shrubbery in the dark, with stars overhead, and snatches of song floating on the wind from every quarter, giving a sense of Christmas joy.

But they needed to be heard at a distance. Near at hand the children, then utterly untrained in voice, sang like ballad-singers, generally—

> While shepherds watched their flocks by night;

but sometimes that notable carol where Lazarus is described among the dogs—

> He had no strength to drive them off,
> And so—and so they licked his sores;

and finally 'Divers' (as he was always called) sits on a serpent's knee!

The shrill thin voices of the children were only ignorantly irreverent, but there were parties of boisterous lads or idle men as ignorant, more profane, and sometimes half-tipsy, and on the way to be entirely so.

The practice had to be reformed. Picturesqueness is apt not to bear close inspection, and propriety and reverence must be enforced even through primness and a little hard-heartedness. So now the children of a fit age are taught well-chosen carols, and go round under the surveillance of the master and mistress, and the money-box is divided at the end, and produces more than the chance pence thrown at haphazard and not at all after the change is exhausted; and the children, who do not remember the old days of license, greatly delight in their rounds.

Charlotte M. Yonge

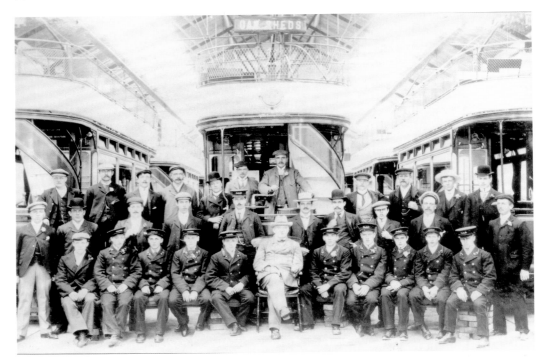

LIGHT RAILWAY STAFF, COWPLAIN

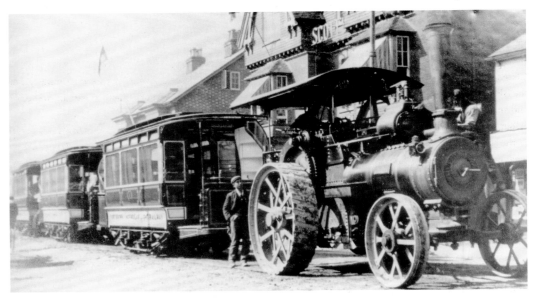

TRAMS, WATERLOOVILLE

PORTSMOUTH TRAMS

The Provincial Tramway Company is moving, too, on Parliamentary lines, and seeks for power to use electricity as a motive force over the whole of its system at Portsmouth. The current is to be conveyed by overhead wires, and permission will be asked by the Company to erect generating stations at each end of the town, and to use the electric current supplied by the Corporation. The Company will thus have two strings to its bow in the matter of motive power. It further seeks for authority to sell the electric current to the Corporation. In the event of the

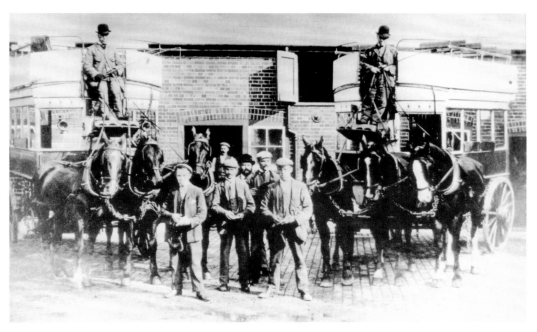

HORSE BUSES, WATERLOOVILLE

Bill becoming law—and at present there is no talk of opposition to it—an arrangement which would be mutually beneficial may be expected between the Company and the Electric Lighting Committee of the Corporation.

Hampshire Telegraph, 23 November 1895

SOUTHSEA AND PORTSMOUTH

Clarence Pier, where all day long, with never-ending interest, they watch the steamers going to and returning from the Isle of Wight; they delight in the white-winged yachts that skim in and out of Portsmouth Harbour; they talk, and smoke, and eat chocolate, and flirt; they invest innumerable pence on the automatic boxes. . .

'But there is something more to be seen on the Clarence Pier, afternoon and evening, than the harmless nonsense of the seaside. Here come popular artists from London to sing at first-class concerts, and here may be heard the magnificent string band of the Royal Marine Artillery. In fact, Southsea boasts two piers, one at the Eastney end, and one at the Portsmouth end, and both piers are devoted to good music and automatic machines. Between the piers is a kind of mutual Campo Santo, facing the sea, where they erect monuments, tombstones, and cenotaphs to distinguished men beloved of Southsea and its immediate district. It is a strange fancy to mix up boats and bathing-machines, restaurants and lollypops, with seaside tombstones and granite memorials; but I do not think it is an inappropriate place for such humble and affectionate memorials of good men and great deeds of the deep.

'Municipally considered, I don't suppose that there are two smarter sea-coast places in the south than Southsea and Portsmouth. Everything for the public service, such as cabs and lighting and good roads and order, is admirably managed at both places; but I very much doubt if "old salts" would recognize the Portsmouth of Charles Dickens and Captain Marryat. . . in the new, smart, red-bricked Portsmouth, with its magnificent barracks, park, and recreation grounds, its imposing town hall—one of the finest in the kingdom—in the Portsmouth up-to-date, which only requires a new railway station to make it perfect.

Clement Scott

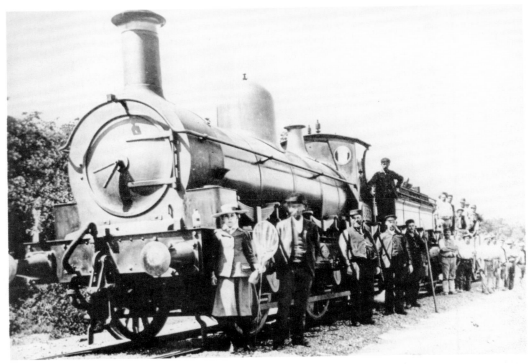

WORKS TRAIN, LITCHFIELD

THE COMING OF THE RAILWAY

When the railway to Portsmouth was completed Liphook was deserted by the travelling world, and an interval of dulness and stagnation followed for it, when the lovers of the picturesque and the seekers after health resorts had not as yet discovered the attractions of the forest lands, to which the eyes of Wilkes and Cobbett had been sealed.

The condition of the 'Anchor' in 1865 is thus described by Grantley Berkeley. 'Time was when. . . the roar of wheels and the cries of 'first and second turn out,' either 'up or down,' rang through the merry air, and kept the locality in loud and continuous bustle night and day. Now, however, the glory of the roadside inn was gone. . . There were the long ranges of stables, once filled by steeds of every step and temper. . . . They reminded me of my own. Where in my full stalls, twenty goodly steeds used to feed, little else than a mouse stirs now.... A broken broom, covered with very ancient cobwebs, lay under one manger, and the remnants of a stable bucket under another. Farmers came in and farmers went out occasionally and tied up their horses anywhere; so that all the tumbling down stalls were dirty, and the whole thing given up to dreary desolation. . . . No smart waiter, with a napkin twisted round his thumb, came forth to my summons; the few people in the house looked like broken-down farming men and women, and seemed to be occupied in the selfish discussion of their own tap.

Under more skilful management the ancient inn speedily regained some of its earlier attractiveness and comfort, and summer guests filled—often to overflowing—the rooms that still bore the names of the royal visitors of old, but the twenty-six coaches and public vans that used to pass through Liphook, in the twenty-four hours were only fading memories now, and for a while there was little to be seen on the great highway but here and there a farm waggon, or for a short time longer the little carts of the fish dealers from the coast to which the panting dogs were harnessed. The housewives made themselves their weekly visits to the village shop, and grocers' carts were as yet unknown in the countryside. The growth of Liphook was of course arrested; population was now to gather round the Railway Station, still further from the centre of the parish, and a new road to connect the two groups was made by the owner of Chiltelee in lieu of a right-of-way across his park, which had connected the Wheatsheaf and White Hart with the Haslemere Road.

W. W. Capes

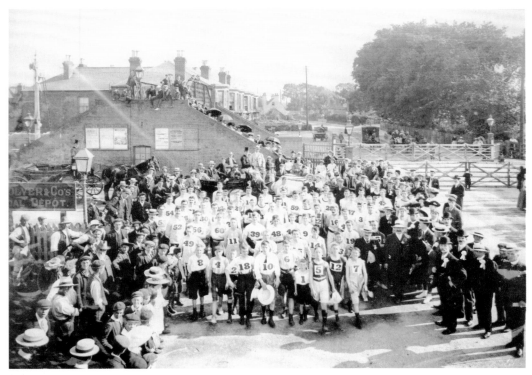

SHOPS ASSISTANTS' WALK, COSHAM

HAMPSHIRE WORDS

Caddle, untidy condition.

'In he comes when I'm all of a caddle.'

To *stabble*, to walk about aimlessly, or in the wet.

'Now, Miss, don't you come stabbling in and out when I am scouring.'

Or,

'I can't come stabbling down that there dirty lane, or I should be all of a muck.'

Want, mole.

Chiselbob, woodlouse; also called a cud-worm, and, rolled in a pill, put down the throat of a cow to promote the restoration of her cud, which she was supposed to have lost.

Gowk, cuckoo.

Fuzz-Buzz, traveller's joy.

Palmer, caterpillar.

Dish-washer, water-wagtail.

Chink, chaffinch.

Long-tailed caper, long-tailed tit.

Yaffil, green woodpecker.

'The yaffil laughed loud.'

Smellfox, anemone.

Dead men's fingers, orchis.

Granny's night-cap, water avens.

Jacob's ladder, Solomon's seal.

Lady's slipper, Prunella vulgaris.

Poppy, foxglove.

To *routle*, to rummage (like a pig in straw).

To *terrify*, to worry or disturb.

'Poor old man, the children did terrify him so, he is gone into the Union.'

Wind-list, white streak of faint cloud across a blue sky, showing the direction of the wind.

Shuffler, man employed about a farmyard.

Randy go, uproar.

'I could not sleep for that there randy go they was making.'

Pook, a haycock.

All of a pummy, all of a moulter, because it was so very brow, describing the condition of a tree, which shattered as it fell because it was brow, i.e. brittle.

Leer, empty, generally said of hunger.—See German.

Hulls, chaff. The chaff of oats; used to be in favour for stuffing mattresses.

Heft, Weight.

To *huck*, to push or pull out. Scotch (howk).

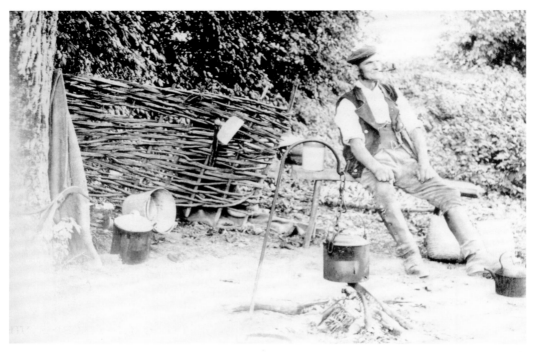

HURDLE MAKER, ALTON

Stook, the foundation of a bee hive.

Pe-art, bright, lively, the original word *bearht* for both bright and pert.

Loo (or *lee*), sheltered.

Steady, slow.

'She is so steady I can't do nothing with her.'

Kickety, said of a one-sided wheel-barrow that kicked up (but this may have been invented for the nonce).

Pecty, covered with little spots of decay.

Fecty, defective throughout—both used in describing apples or potatoes.

Hedge-picks, sloes.

Hags or *aggarts*, haws.

Rauch, smoke (comp. German and Scotch).

Pond-keeper, dragon-fly.

Stupid, ill-conditioned.

To plim, to swell, as bacon boiled.

To side up, to put tidy.

Logie, poorly, out-of-sorts.

Charlotte M. Yonge

FIRST KNOWN WHEN LOST

I never had noticed it until
'Twas gone,—the narrow copse
Where now the woodman lops
The last of the willows with his bill.

It was not more than a hedge o'ergrown.
One meadow's breadth away
I passed it day by day.
Now the soil is bare as a bone,

And black betwixt two meadows green,
Though fresh-cut faggot ends
Of hazel make some amends
With a gleam as if flowers they had been.

Strange it could have hidden so near!
And now I see as I look
That the small winding brook,
A tributary's tributary rises there.

Edward Thomas

DOCKYARD EMPLOYMENT

The sailmakers in Portsmouth Dockyard have a genuine cause of complaint in the somewhat cavalier treatment to which they have been recently subjected by the authorities of the Yard. It seems that the Admiralty recently issued advertisements for qualified sailmakers, but as the proper rating and the trade rate of pay were not promised, very

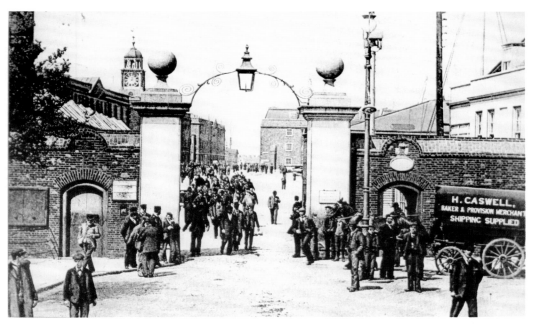

THE DOCKYARD, PORTSMOUTH

few outside men offered their services. On this notice was sent to the ships in commission at the principal home ports, inviting bluejackets to apply for entry as naval sailmakers, but although there was no lack of applications, at Portsmouth only one or two of the men who came forward passed the necessary examination. Orders have now been issued that four or five men will be sent to the sail-loft from the depot every day to undergo a course of instruction in sailmaking. Considering that the Dockyard authorities are entering apprentices to the sailmaking, and that these youths have to be apprenticed for six years, the proposal to qualify men to do the same kind of work in a few months is manifestly unfair. No other trade, it is said, would tolerate such treatment. If sailmakers are wanted in the Navy men should be entered who have passed through their ordinary apprenticeship, and the proper rate of pay should be offered.

Hampshire Telegraph, 15 June 1895

A WEEK'S CHEAP LIVING

'A Labourer's Wife,' writes to the *Evening News* as follows:

I wish to write as the wife of a well-to-do workman of the labour class. We have had hard times this winter— weeks of frost, and no work, and it makes the future a dark outlook. May I stop, however, to thank the Distress Committee, and the public for their admirable and kind efforts to help us now that we are down.

But my object is to ask a question. How may we save for a rainy day? I heard a rich gentleman say only yesterday that 'those people ought to provide for such occasions as the present.'

I am one of those who believe in facing difficulties. This is my position. My husband earns 16s. per week, and I have three children depending upon me. I want to save. I am, and so are my family, total abstainers. How can I reasonably, save, say 1s. per week, and bank it at the Savings Bank? I give you my week's account:—

MONDAY.

Rent, 4s.

Breakfast—Bread and butter, tea and milk, 3½d.

Dinner—Irish stew and rice, 1s.

Tea—Bread and butter, tea and milk, 3½d.

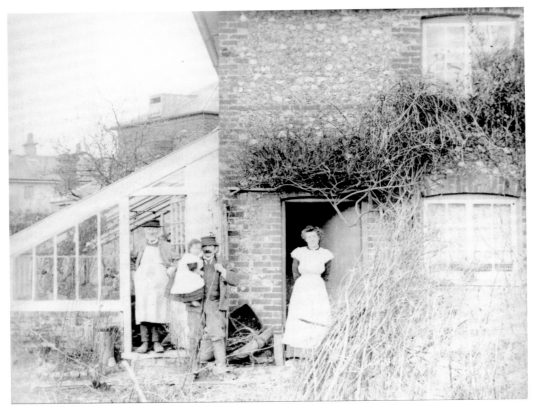

FAMILY, HORNDEAN

TUESDAY.

Breakfast—Bread and herrings, tea and milk, 4d.

Dinner—Pea-soup and bread, 6d.

Tea—Bread and jam, tea and milk, 4½d.

WEDNESDAY.

Breakfast—Bread and butter, tea and milk, 3½d.

Dinner—Pig's fry and potatoes, 7d.

Tea—Bread and butter, tea and milk, 3½d.

THURSDAY.

Breakfast—Bread and treacle, cocoa and milk, 4d.

Dinner—Stewed scraps and potatoes and bread, 1s.

Tea—Bread and butter, tea and milk, 3½d.

FRIDAY.

Breakfast—Bread and butter, cocoa and milk, 4d.

Dinner—Salt fish and potatoes, bread, etc., 10d.

Tea—Bread and butter, tea and milk, 3d.

SATURDAY.

Breakfast—Bread and butter, tea and milk, 3½d.

Dinner—Lentil soup and bread, 6d.; rice (boiled), 3d.

Tea—Bread and butter, tea and milk, 3d.

SUNDAY.

Breakfast—Bread and butter, tea, etc., 3½d.

Dinner—Stewed steak, onions, and potatoes, 'Spotted Dick' pudding, 1s. 6d.

Tea—Bread and jam, tea, etc., 4d.

Coals and oil, 1s.

For clothes, boots, soap, etc., per week, 7d.

Total—16s.

If some kind lady or some good cook will try to live one week, on 16s. per week, deducting 4s. as if for rent, and then write to the papers, it would be such a help. Poor people are not always good cooks, but with an onion, a potato, and a scrap of meat, I can make a nice savoury smell, if it be but a bare bone in the cupboard. Is there any book written for the poor giving particulars how to live on a small sum? If so, Sir, kindly let us know through your valuable paper.

Hampshire Telegraph, 23 February 1895

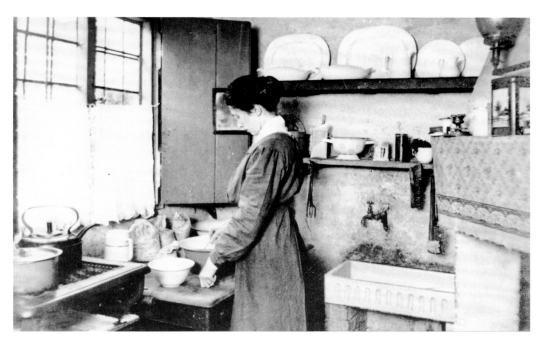

KITCHENS, STOKE COTTAGE, WATERLOOVILLE

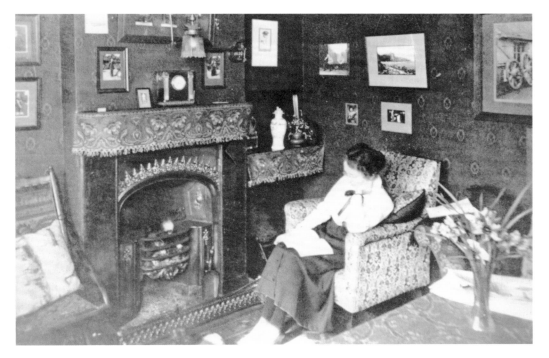

PARLOUR, STOKE COTTAGE, WATERLOOVILLE

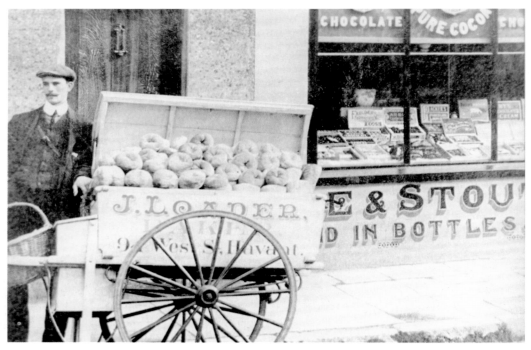

WEST STREET, HAVANT

THE OTTERBOURNE BAKER

Mr William Stainer was a baker. His bread was excellent, and he was also noted for what were called Otterbourne buns, the art of making which seems to have gone with him. They were small fair-complexioned buns, which stuck together in parties of three, and when soaked, expanded to twice or three times their former size. He used to send them once or twice a week to Winchester. But though baking was his profession, he did much besides. He was a real old-fashioned herbalist, and had a curious book on the virtues of plants, and he made decoctions of many kinds, which he administered to those in want of medicine. Before the Poor Law provided Union doctors, medical advice, except at the hospital, was almost out of reach of the poor. Mr and Mrs Yonge, like almost all other beneficent gentlefolks in villages, kept a medicine chest and book, and doctored such cases as they could venture on, and Mr Stainer was in great favour as a practitioner, as many of our elder people can remember. He was exceedingly charitable and kind, and ready to give his help so far as he could. He was a great lover of flowers, and had contrived a sort of little greenhouse over the great oven at the back of his house, and there he used to bring up lovely geraniums and other flowers, which he sometimes sold. He was a deeply religious and devout man, and during an illness of the clerk took his place in Church, which was more important when there was no choir and the singers sat in the gallery. He was very happy in this office, moving about on felt shoes that he might make no noise, and most reverently keeping the Church clean, and watching over it in every way. He also continued in the post of schoolmaster, which at first he had only taken temporarily, and quaintly managing it. He was found setting as a copy 'A blind man's wife needs no paint,' which he defended as 'Proverbs, sir, Proverbs.' Giving up part of his business to his nephew, he still sat up at night baking, for the nephew, he said, was only in the A B C book of baking, and he also had other troubles: there was insanity in his family, and he was much harassed. His kindness and simplicity were sometimes abused. He never had the heart to refuse to lend money, or to deny bread on credit to hopeless debtors; and altogether debts, distress, baking, and watching his sisters all night, and school keeping all day, were too much for him. The first hint of an examination of his school completed the mischief, and he died insane, drowning himself in the canal. It is a sad story, but many of us will remember with affectionate regard the good, kind, quaint, and most excellent little man.

Charlotte M. Yonge

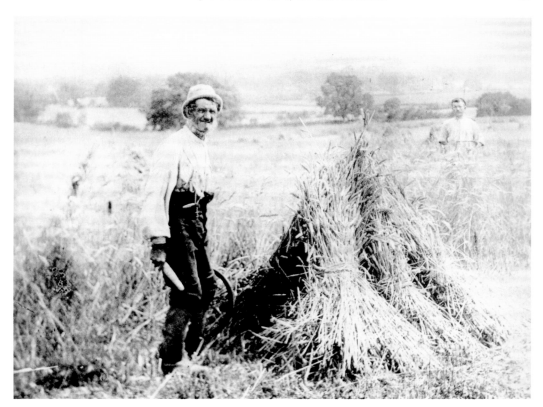

REAPING WHEAT, NEAR ALTON

HARVESTING

Harvest is not quite the parish feast it used to be, when I have known a little maid who had spent some time prosperously in service, begin to weep so pitifully and incessantly at the thought of the delights she was losing, that she had to be restored to her home!

The whole families used to turn out together, to reap and bind, and it was considered 'lucky' if the child, just promoted to reaping, cut herself with the sickle. Even if the top of a finger was cut off, it was speedily joined on with a quid of tobacco.

On worked and feasted the family in its own portions till the last sheaf—beautiful thing—was loaded, and the gladsome shout proclaimed it. Then, still more delightful, the women and children turned out to lease (as they call gleaning), and might be seen plodding home loaded with thin little sheaves artistically tied up with plaited straws, and great bags of ears that had fallen without their stems. Piles of corn were heaped before the houses, but, alas! few housewives either glean or bake now. They depend entirely on the baker's cart.

The joy of harvest has not passed away, and there is less wildness, less temptation therewith, but much picturesqueness is gone. The reaping machine has taken the place of the family, and leaves rows to be gathered and bound up into sheaves, and built up in the rain-repelling arrangements, which happily have never been improved upon.

The shout proclaiming the carrying of the last sheaf rings out in turn from farm to farm, though most of the picturesque observances of the harvest home are dying away before the tramp of the schoolmaster, and still more the squeal and hum of the machine.

Charlotte M. Yonge

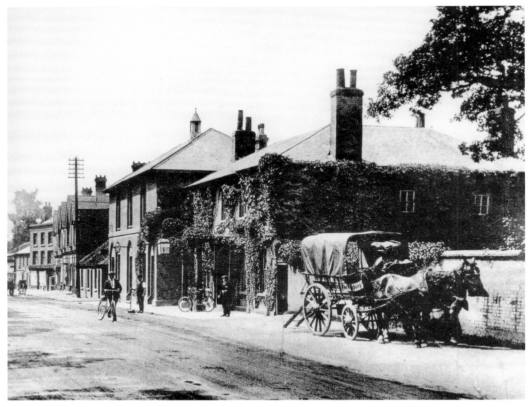

TUMBLE DOWN DICK HOTEL, FARNBOROUGH

THE OTHER

The forest ended. Glad I was
To feel the light, and hear the hum
Of bees, and smell the drying grass
And the sweet mint, because I had come
To an end of forest, and because
Here was both road and inn, the sum
Of what's not forest. But 'twas here
They asked me if I did not pass
Yesterday this way? 'Not you? Queer.'
'Who then? and slept here?' I felt fear.

I learnt his road and, ere they were
Sure I was I, left the dark wood
Behind, kestrel and woodpecker,
The inn in the sun, the happy mood
When first I tasted sunlight there.
I travelled fast, in hopes I should
Outrun that other. What to do
When caught, I planned not. I pursued
To prove the likeness, and, if true,
To watch until myself I knew.

I tried the inns that evening
Of a long gabled high-street grey,
Of courts and outskirts, travelling
An eager but a weary way;
In vain. He was not there. Nothing
Told me that ever till that day
Had one like me entered those doors
Save once. That time I dared: 'You may
Recall'—but never-foam-less shores
Make better friends than those dull boors.

Edward Thomas

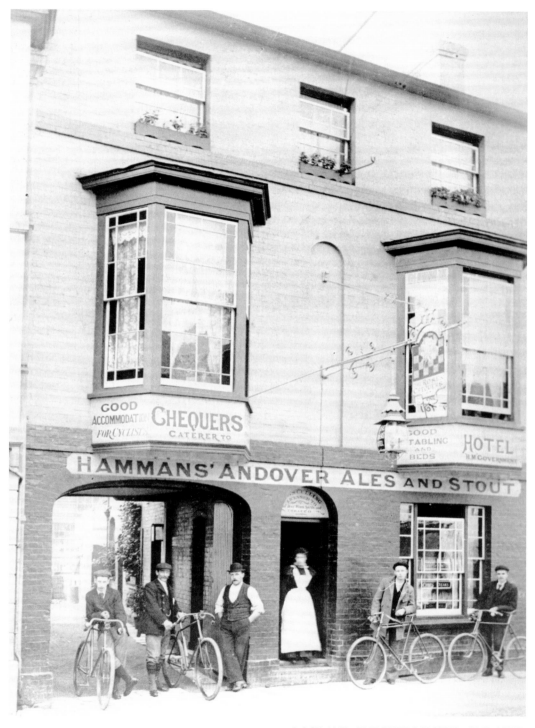

ROSE AND CHEQUERS HOTEL, ANDOVER

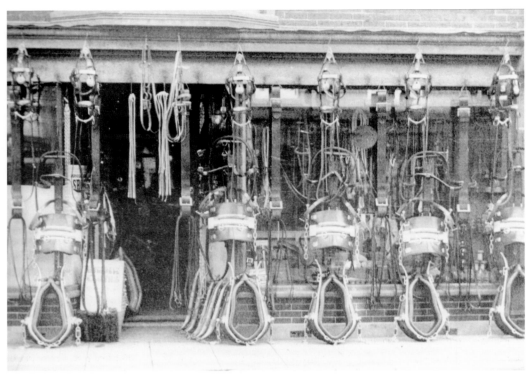

SADDLER, HAVANT

VILLAGE INDUSTRIES

The knowledge acquired by men used to general farm work from boyhood makes the farm labourer's a skilled profession, and worthy of much more respect than has been accorded it. There is one old man in the village now, who till well over eighty could turn his hand to an infinite variety of jobs—and look after people's gardens and his vegetable plot in his spare time. At harvest time he worked in the fields with the mechanical reaper and binder, setting up 'stooks' with a rapidity which beat the younger men, and kept up with the machine from morning till evening.

Another job, hedging, occupied him in season; with him it is no mere hacking down to a level. He selected and bent, split and twisted with a skill that is becoming rare, and his hedge was a work of art, with the beauty that is the fruit of good workmanship, and a foresight that can look to results as yet unseen. And so on, through the year, as the months with their varied tasks come and go, his knowledge, wisdom and patience were called upon and did not fail.

When he was over 80, the bales of a rick—not of his building—fell on a girl, to whose aid he ran. More bales fell and 'flattened' them both. He was brought home all sprains and bruises, and told to rest in bed. In a few days he was about again, and very soon at work. 'I don't like to bide in bed, I don't. I be better when I gets about,' was his explanation. He has a store of memories from his long life, the whole of which has been spent in the village, and a rich humour flavours his comments on them. He remembers the visits of Joseph Arch in the 1870s and '80s and the meetings of agricultural labourers, who thronged to hear him. Joseph Arch was, he reports, 'not very tall', but he 'could speak'. Asked if any trouble arose from Arch's work, a twinkle came into his eye: 'Not here, Mu'm. But some of the gentry didn't like 'un, that they didn't, for see he was after raising our wages. Yes, that was what he was after.'

A sturdy character of a past age was the rope and harness-maker whose thatched brick-and-flint cottage was also his shop, and stood next to the orchard where he had a long enough run to twist his ropes. Hand-made ropes such as were then made are no longer in demand, and with the increase of motor transport and mechanical farming a man would be hard put to it to live on harness-making. His pride in the harness he made was justified.

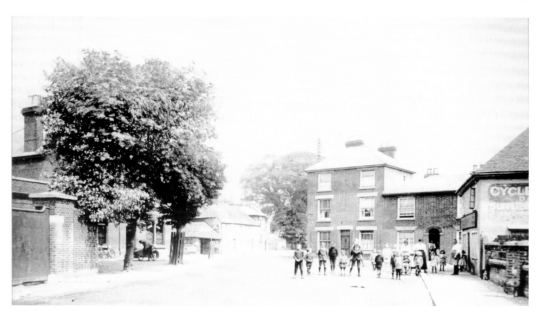

MAIN ROAD, PORTCHESTER

The polished leather was as shining as the brass ornaments that adorned it. Every piece was finished to the highest degree. The counter inside his window was always worth stopping to examine as completed pieces were placed there when waiting to be called for. When the rope-maker died, his rope-walk was taken into the neighbouring garden, and the harness-making came to an end.

Unlike the harness-maker's, the work of the blacksmith has changed but not dwindled. The smithy in which he works is mid-way up the village street. It was built for a smithy and has long been in use. Its floor is made of round blocks of hard wood, standing upright and let into the floor side by side. These are less trying for the feet than stone or cement, and do not get as hot from the fire, so that the air is not so dry, and the reflection of heat is lessened.

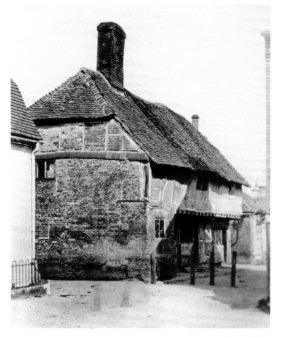

Fifty years ago the cobbler not only cobbled but really made shoes—or rather, perhaps, sturdy boots for rough country roads, also wooden soled clogs. His shop was a centre of information and gossip. Men gathered there, and talked while he worked at his bench in the window.

Near the school there was a most picturesque bakery and shop in a cottage, low-thatched and white-washed, with redbrick floors. The shop portion was entered by steps which led down into a spacious and cool, square room, low-ceilinged, fitted with shelves and counters, on which everything was orderly and from which everything seemed obtainable. The bakery, with huge brick ovens beside the fireplace, was next door, and the sweet aroma of baked bread from ovens heated with burning faggots pervaded the place.

Kathleen E. Innes

ODIHAM

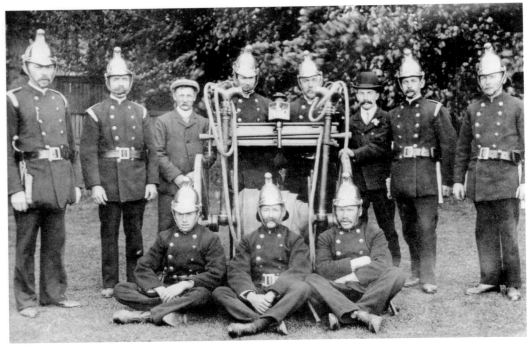

FIRE BRIGADE, WATERLOOVILLE

FIRE AT WATERLOOVILLE

A serious fire, which resulted in several thousands of pounds' worth of damage, occurred on Tuesday night at Waterlooville, near Portsmouth.

It appears that shortly before eleven o'clock one of the men in the employ of Mr Pennekett, baker and grocer, heard the cracking and falling of slates. He immediately investigated the matter, and found that the back portion of the premises was on fire. Mr Pennekett sen., and his son were away, but Mrs Pennekett and her child were in bed. They were aroused, and made a hurried exit into the street. The fire appeared to be of considerable extent, and the whole village soon turned out, everyone being thoroughly alarmed. There are no fire appliances in the village, though a fire-engine of some sort has long been felt to be a necessity. Mr Rastall, therefore, undertook to go to Havant on a bicycle, and did so, giving the alarm to the brigade, which at once turned out. He occupied a considerable time in accomplishing the journey, owing to the bad stony state of the roads. A second messenger followed in a trap and took back the captain of the brigade, Mr Stent, with a hose, which was at once attached to a hydrant, a good supply of water being thus delivered on to the fire.

The flames had spread rapidly, and had taken a good hold of the back of Mr Pennekett's premises and extended to the adjoining buildings. The whole of the people in the village watched the progress of the flames with anxiety. Mr Wadham, who lives in the Exchange, next door to Pennekett's, got his—family into the street, but was reassured on finding that the wind blew away from his shop. Mrs Pennekett and the child were taken in by Mr Wadham and given shelter. It was not very long before the shop of Mr Long, butcher, which adjoins Pennekett's, was ablaze, and the dwelling house of Mrs Carter also caught.

SAD DOMESTIC LOSSES.

The Havant Fire Brigade arrived shortly before twelve o'clock, and at once got to work. Their efforts prevented the fire spreading, but it looked so likely that other houses would catch that several people moved their portable goods into the street. The roof of Mr Pennekett's shop gradually burst through and collapsed, and when the fire was finally got under, after two hours' hard work, three buildings involved were completely burnt out, almost every article of stock at Mr Penneketts was destroyed, but the books and cash-box were saved. Mrs Long lost

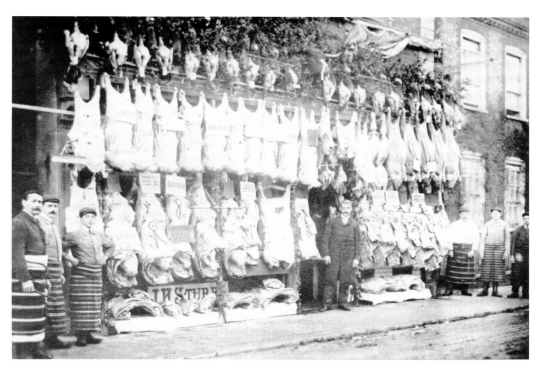

BUTCHERS SHOP, WATERLOOVILLE

absolutely everything, including every article of her wardrobe except the dressing-gown in which she escaped into the street, and she had to be supplied with clothing by the neighbours. In the shop only a lamb chop was left. Not even the vestige of a chair or table was to be found.

The property belongs to Mr G. S. Lancaster, J.P., and is insured. At present the exact cause of the outbreak is unknown, but it is supposed that some straw was ignited by wood ashes.

Hampshire Telegraph, 1 June 1895

HAMPSHIRE HOGS

In the New Forest there is a period called Pannage time, when the cottagers have a right, for six weeks, to turn out their swine to enjoy the harvest under the trees.

'Hampshire hogs' thus sometimes have begun upon hogs' food. I do not know whether the Hampshire man is more devoted to his pig than the natives of other counties, but it certainly fills an important place in the family possessions. Scarcely a house is without a tidy pigstye, the resort of the ruminating master, pipe in mouth, in Sunday leisure. A woman dying of a long illness expressed her mournful regrets to her clergyman that she had never seen the present pig, adding that her husband said that, if he had known in time how much she wished it, he would have carried it upstairs, but now it was too big and heavy.

So the pig is the family pet and pride until the day when the parish executioner comes.

Here in Hampshire the further destination of the bacon pig, after being cut up into joints and salted, is to be smoked in a chimney adapted for the purpose, but only from a wood fire, and we found it impossible to induce cottagers to abstain from coal. The smoking is done specially at the village shop. . . and, though we here respect the pork well-roasted and furrowed with crackle, and the fair delicate salt pork leg, we hold that bacon is no bacon unless smoked.

It is not by any means still the only flesh food of the labourer. . . Now there is more use of tinned meats, and carts from butchers come round and carry on a small traffic, giving more variety, as well as other carts of cheap fish.

Charlotte M. Yonge

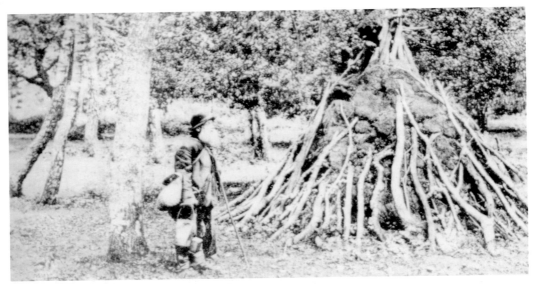

'BRUSHER' MILLS, SNAKE CATCHER

PEOPLE OF THE NEW FOREST

It must be borne in mind that the Forest area has a considerable population composed of commoners, squatters, private owners, who have inherited or purchased lands originally filched from the Forest; and of a large number of persons who reside mostly in the villages, and are private residents, publicans, shopkeepers, and lodging-house keepers. All these people have one object in common—to get as much as they can out of the Forest. It is true that a large proportion of them, especially those who live in the villages, which are now rapidly increasing their populations, are supposed not to have any Forest rights; but they do as a fact get something out of it; and we may say that, generally, all the people in the Forest dine at one table, and all get a helping out of most of the dishes going, though the first and biggest helpings are for the favoured guests.

The New Forest people are, in fact, just what circumstances have made them. Like all organized beings, they are the creatures of, and subject to, the conditions they exist in; and they cannot be other than they are—namely, parasites on the Forest. And, what is more, they cannot be educated, or preached, or worried out of their ingrained parasitical habits and ways of thought. They have had centuries—long centuries—of practise to make them cunning, and the effect of more stringent regulations than those now in use would only be to polish and put a better edge on that weapon which Nature has given them to fight with.

The Forest has been known and loved by a limited number of persons always; the general public have only discovered it in recent years. For one visitor twenty years ago there are scores, probably hundreds, today. And year by year, as motoring becomes more common, and as cycling from being general grows, as it will, to be universal, the flow of visitors to the Forest will go on at an ever-increasing rate, and the hundreds of today will be thousands in five years' time. With these modern means of locomotion, there is no more attractive spot than this hundred and fifty square miles of level country which contains the most beautiful forest scenery in England. And as it grows in favour in all the country as a place of recreation and refreshment, the subject of its condition and management, and the ways of its inhabitants, will receive an increased attention. The desire will grow that it shall not be spoilt, either by the authorities or the residents, that it shall not be turned into townships and plantations, nor be starved, nor its wild life left to be taken and destroyed by any one and every one. It will be seen that the 'rights' I have spoken of, with the unwritten laws and customs which are kept more or less in the dark, are in conflict with the better and infinitely more important rights of the people generally—of the whole nation. Once all this becomes common knowledge, that which some now regard as a mere dream, a faint hope, something too remote for us to concern ourselves about, will all at once appear to us as a practical object—something to be won by fighting, and certainly worth fighting for.

W. H. Hudson

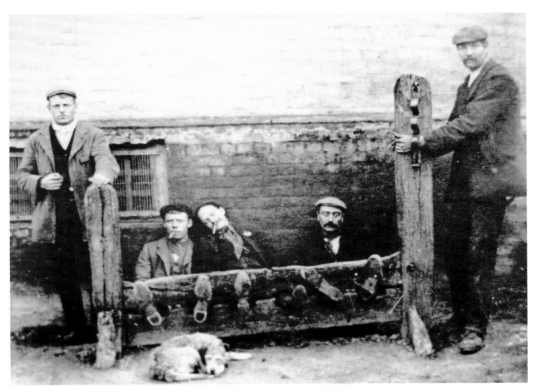

STOCKS AND WHIPPING POST, ODIHAM

CUSTOMS

A tenth child, if all the former ones are living, is baptized with a sprig of myrtle in his cap, and the clergyman was supposed to charge himself with his education.

If possible, a baby was short-coated on Good Friday, to ensure not catching cold.

The old custom (now gone out) was that farmers should send their men to church on Good Friday. They used all to appear in their rough dirty smock-frocks and go back to work again. Some (of whom it would never have been expected) would fast all day.

The 29th of May is still called Shick-shack day—why has never been discovered. There must have been some observance earlier than the Restoration, though oak-apples are still worn on that day, and with their oak sprays are called Shick-shack.

On St Clement's Day, the 23rd of November, explosions of gunpowder are made on country blacksmiths' anvils. It is viewed as the blacksmiths' holiday. The accepted legend is that St Clement was drowned with an anchor hung to his neck, and that his body was found in a submarine temple, from which the sea receded every seven years for the benefit of pilgrims. Thus he became the patron of anchor forgers, and thence of smiths in general. Charles Dickens, in *Great Expectations* describes an Essex blacksmith as working to a chant, the *refrain* of which was 'Old Clem.' I have heard the explosions at Hursley before 1860, but more modern blacksmiths despise the custom. At Twyford, however, the festival is kept, and at the dinner a story is read that after the Temple was finished, Solomon feasted all the artificers except the blacksmiths, but they appeared, and pointed out all that they had done in the way of necessary work, on which they were included with high honour.

St Thomas's Day, 21st December, is still at Otterbourne held as the day for 'gooding,' when each poor house-mother can demand sixpence from the well-to-do towards her Christmas dinner.

Charlotte M. Yonge

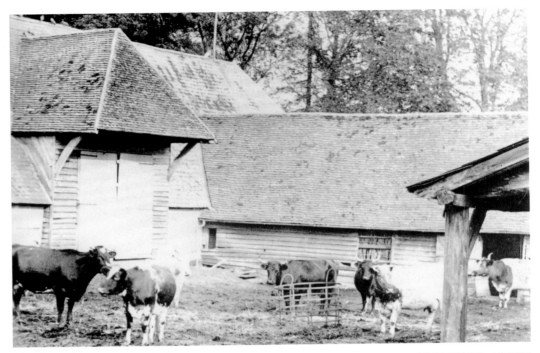

FARMYARD, ALTON

SUNNY MAY

At midday then along the lane
Old Jack Noman appeared again,
Jaunty and old, crooked and tall,
And stopped and grinned at me over the wall,
With a cowslip bunch in his button-hole
And one in his cap. Who could say if his roll
Came from flints in the road, the weather, or ale?
He was welcome as the nightingale.
Not an hour of the sun had been wasted on Jack.
'I've got my Indian complexion back'
Said he. He was tanned like a harvester,
Like his short clay pipe, like the leaf and bur
That clung to his coat from last night's bed,
Like the ploughland crumbling red.
Fairer flowers were none on the earth
Than his cowslips wet with the dew of their birth,
Or fresher leaves than the cress in his basket.

Edward Thomas

WINTER WORK ON THE FARM

Pant, pant! Cough, cough! That noise tells of ploughing. There is an engine at each end of the adjoining field, and a little plough travelling up and down between them in the furrow, apparently of its own accord. Happily there are some farms still left which afford the pleasant sight of the sleek horses plodding before their ploughs, all the better if there be a dappled gray to show out on the rich brown earth of a sloping field.

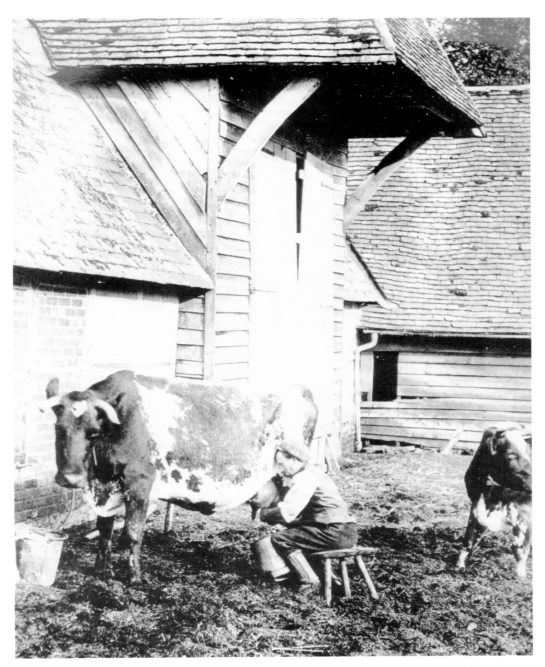

MILKING, ALTON

But the measured thump, thump of the flail on the barn floor, which warmed the labourer on winter days, and kept up his pay, that is a sound which the younger generation have never heard; nor have they seen the curious winnowing machine, with its four fans of canvas which used to revolve in the barns.

The threshing machine, with its engine and lengthy apparatus, makes its rounds among the farms, and its whirr is the familiar sound.

Charlotte M. Yonge

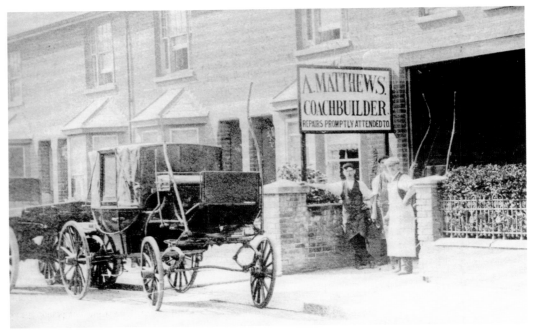

COACHBUILDER, WINCHESTER

THE EARTHQUAKE

From statements to hand it would seem that the earthquake at 5.30 on Thursday morning was distinctly felt by persons resident in various parts of Winchester. The effects as described by several people were the oscillations of the bed, the rattling of crockery, and the shaking of furniture; while in some cases it was found that small articles which had been placed on tables at night were found on the floor in the morning. This shock was also felt at Itchen Abbas. There were two distinct vibrations. A lady at the Rectory was awoke by the shutter of her room rattling, the floor undulating, and the door creaking on its hinges. The underground rumbling was very marked. She knew at once that it was an earthquake. Some of the cottagers also heard noises and were shaken, but in one instance it was put down to rats. The dogs howled, and cocks crowed, being evidently alarmed. Several persons in Yateley and Sandhurst were awakened by a rumbling of the earth and rattling of the doors, &c. Strange to say no one at Eversley, 1½ miles off, has yet reported hearing it. It was felt by people at Minley also.

Hampshire Chronicle, 19 December 1896

THE EMSWORTH WEEK

The sports at Emsworth opened on Monday with every promise of success. The residents seemed to vie with each other in raising the tone of the town, and the neighbourhood looked even gayer than on the occasion of the Queen's Jubilee. The streets were decorated with flags stretched from side to side, while several of the shopkeepers had embellished their business premises with ornamental shields, flowers, evergreens, &c. In the Square was placed a high pole, upon which were hoisted the Union Jack and about a dozen strings of smaller flags, the latter spreading to the windows of different houses near by. At the entrance to King-street there was an arch of evergreens, decorated with flowers, and in the distance could be seen several lines of flags stretched across the road. The mail cart show was the first attraction. This was held in a meadow at the side of Dr Palmer Stephenson's residence, where about two thousand persons assembled. The meadow was decorated for the occasion with festooned flags. There were about fifty mail carts entered, and the judges (Lady Robert Bruce, Hon Lady Craufurd, and Mrs J. E. Cox) had an arduous task in deciding which was the best, so pretty were the exhibits. The first prize, a gold bangle, presented by Mrs C. P Boyd, was awarded to Mr J. A. Napier Martin,

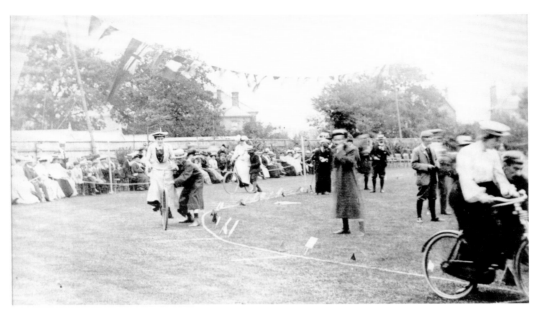

CYCLE CLUB, EMSWORTH

of West Leigh. The second, a gold brooch, given by Dr Stevens, was won by Mrs C. P Boyd; the third, a silk umbrella, the gift of Mrs Hall King, by Mrs Cooper of Emsworth; the fourth, a doll from Mrs Guildford Sprigg by Mrs Haynes of Warblington. Subsequently a water carnival was held on the pond known as Bridge Foot, and when the procession of illuminated boats took place the scene was one of magnificent grandeur. There were about twenty-five boats in the procession and the judges were Admiral Singer, Capt. Fredericks, R.N., and Mr G. P. Martin, R.N. The competition was keen. Mr Mosdell's boat represented a house prettily curtained, and having on the roof the legend, 'Success to our town.' Another boat was manned by coastguardsmen dressed in white, and the flotilla also included a Chinese boat illuminated with lanterns. The judges' awards were announced by Dr Lockhart Stephens, one of the hon. secretaries, as follows:—Bridle boat, Mr A. Agate, 1st; Arctic boat, Misses Crallen, 2nd; and May Pole, Mrs Graham Pigott, 3rd. As the procession passed around the pond, the Royal Marine Artillery band played 'Rule Britannia,' which was answered by some of the musicians on one of the boats striking up 'A life on the ocean wave.' Just as the procession of boats concluded, Messrs James Pain and Sons, of London, gave a magnificent pyrotechnic display. The night being dark, but fine, the fireworks were seen to great advantage. The band of the Royal Marine Artillery, conducted by Mr A. Williams, Mus. Bac., Oxon., played a selection of music at the afternoon entertainment, and also on the banks of the Millpond.

The second day of the Emsworth Week opened with weather anything but promising, a circumstance which tended not only to damp the ground but also the spirits of the promoters of the sports. The cricket match arranged between Priory Park and Westbourne had to be abandoned after the visitors had gone to the wickets and scored five runs. At five o'clock, however, the rain was practically over. An entertainment was held at the Emsworth Rectory, the spacious grounds of which were kindly thrown open by the, Revd H. Guilford for an evening concert and garden fete. The band of the Royal Marine Artillery played a well-arranged programme of music. At the end of the lawn a large tent had been erected, where refreshments were dispensed by Mrs George Hall King, Mrs W. Foster, Miss Stephens, and other ladies. In an adjoining meadow Mr H. A. Dixon and friends, dressed in coster garb, had a cocoanut shy, where a brisk trade was done. Mrs H. A. Dixon and a lady friend donated the habiliments of the gipsy class and vended miscellaneous wares. Those who contributed to the concert programme were Miss Lina Carr, Mrs Hooker Wix, Mr Warwick Grey, and Mr Dudley Hughes. The second part of the entertainment consisted of a series of tableaux vivants, with appropriate music by the band.

Hampshire Telegraph, 25 August 1894

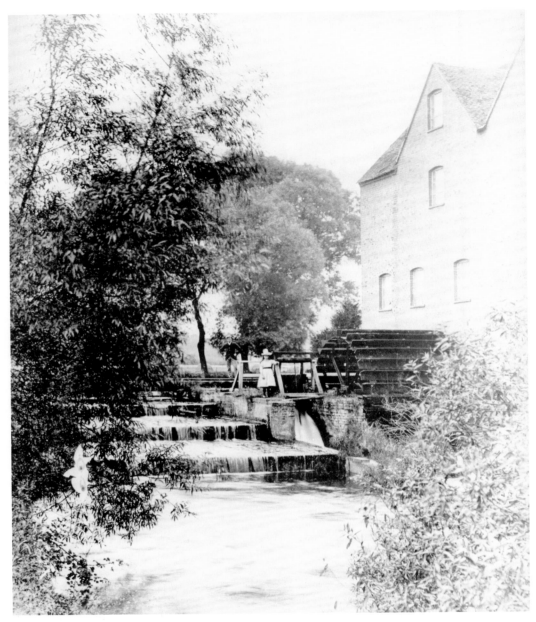

UPPER MILL, BEDHAMPTON

THE MILL-POND

The sun blazed while the thunder yet
Added a boom:
A wagtail flickered bright over
The mill-pond's gloom:

Less than the cooing in the alder
Isles of the pool
Sounded the thunder through that plunge
Of waters cool.

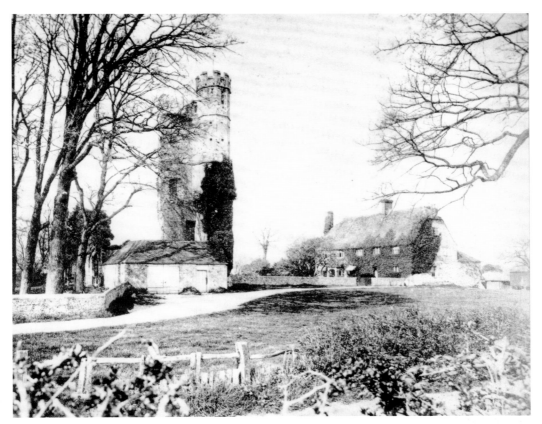

WARBLINGTON CASTLE

Scared starlings on the aspen tip
Past the black mill
Outchattered the stream and the next roar
Far on the hill.

Edward Thomas

LIFE IN A HAMPSHIRE VILLAGE

Short as the time is since I came here, it is long enough to have seen pretentious folk give up their farms, while some who began as labourers have become thriving small cultivators. In one case a legacy enabled the family to buy one cow. Wife and daughters were not above driving her to the common for pasture, or learning to make the best butter. Now they have seven cows and pasture of their own. Another family of brothers rented jointly a small farm, which they have worked so profitably as to be able to increase their holdings and to invest in valuable agricultural machines for their own use and for hire. They do the real labour of their land, and their families occupy the comfortable house together.

Simple labourers are to me more sympathetic than their masters. The impossibility of pretension, and the calmness with which they live by daily bread, dignify in character what is lacking in education.

Our village affords exceptional advantages in its spacious common of six hundred acres, where each cottager may pasture two cows. This pasture land lies on the top of the hill, in glades sheltered by groves of oak, and bordered by copses of nutwood and thickets of fern. Here they may gather nitches of deadwood and dried fern, plentiful nuts, wild plums and berries, even Alpine strawberries in abundance. If by rare chance they perceive the beauty of the earth, they know why this place calls all wanderers to return.

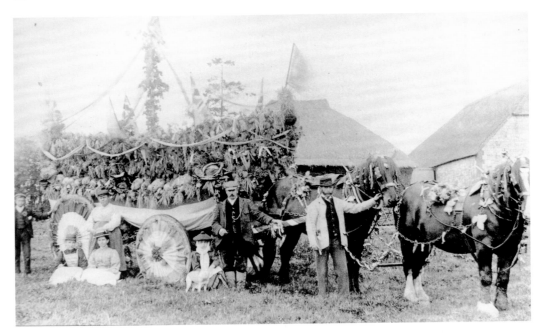

DECORATED WAGON, BINSTEAD

Below in the village are the allotments, where each cottager may hire, for two shillings and sevenpence a year, a strip of well-lying land, two hundred feet long and fifteen wide. The allotments lie together, separated by narrow grass paths. Here the labourer, after his long day's work for hire, never less than ten hours, works for an hour or two in the evening and gets potatoes and greens for his household.

The labourers' cottages, near at hand, are little whitened huts, curiously compounded of bricks, timber, hurdles, and mortar (called expressively wattle and daub), and covered with thatch. From a distance they are scarcely distinguishable from the ricks. Two or three tiny rooms shelter large families living by unceasing toil; toil which has no reward but daily bread and hardly enough of that. And yet, in this narrow home, affection and self-sacrifice find room enough. Many a man with eight or nine children receives only eleven shillings a week for daily work from dawn to dark. A little extra money for harvest pays the rent and spare fuel. They must begin their life of toil so soon as school board requirements are satisfied, and very often have to trudge two or three miles to their work, which begins at seven o'clock. Boys have only sixpence a day, with thirty shillings at Michaelmas. What wonder that sometimes they look rather lounging and listless, with their growing youth's hunger never quite satisfied at the crowded home table.

At harvest or haymaking they often find work seven or ten miles distant, where they sleep under a hedge and walk home occasionally for cooked food. Meat is certainly not tasted except on Sundays.

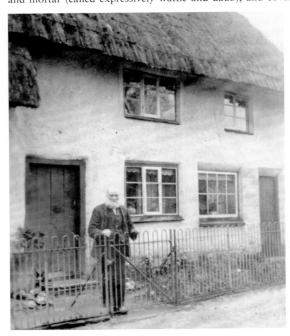

COTTAGE, UPPER CLATFORD

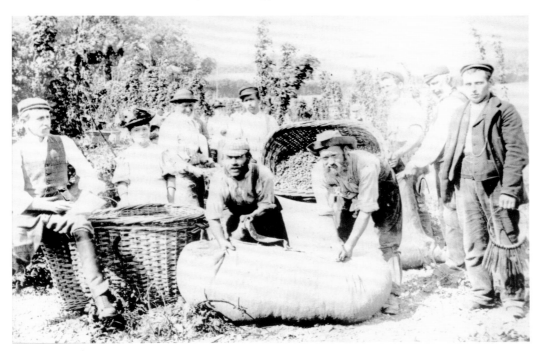

HOP PICKERS, ALTON

The only amusement for girls is the fête of their Friendly Society, and that brings many young servants home from their places in towns for a summer holiday. Fresh cotton frocks and straw hats set off their pretty faces and figures. These people are often very handsome, even beautiful, but at forty a workman has stiff limbs and gait, and his face is lined as by heavy years. There is little chance for them to seek a neighbourhood of higher wages. Moving their little households to any distance would be a ruinous expense, but the children at least go out into the world at twelve years old, perhaps far away, and parents grow into easier, though solitary, old age. There are often little extras to their small wages, in their pig, or a hatching of ducks or chickens. If a man's pig dies a natural death he expects us all to help him buy another. On the common they gather stores of dead wood and small fuel and dried bracken. Even the aged blind woman is led up the hill and breathes the fresh sea air in that higher atmosphere, returning with a load that almost hides her bent figure.

Dried fern is good bedding for the pig and tender plants. Then, too, there is liberal gleaning and, in autumn, nuts, wild berries, and mushrooms may be gathered to sell, and women are paid a little for turning hay and weeding. The last work of the old labourer is road-mending, and it is strange to see those who are past all active work sitting on the roadside breaking flint. Any work is happier than idleness, for without mental activity it is impossible to be idle amusingly. It is touching to note the frequent deaths of aged people at their work or in the field. Touching, too, to note the nameless mounds on the hill above the church, where the long grass is neatly trimmed and fresh flowers constantly laid by those who remember. Saturday evening is the favourite time for tending these memorials. There to-day came an old man, far in the eighties, carrying up the steep path a can of water for the newly planted flower on his wife's grave. He said: 'I am so glad she did not have to live after me.'

I love to see the harvest work. There is a grand cornfield quite near. Down through the green lane under cool shade from overhanging ash, between walls of clematis and honeysuckle in bloom, we come suddenly into unusual stir. Little children, tidily dressed, are in charge of thirsty babies and of baskets with refreshing drinks, not for the babies—bottles wrapped in big leaves and kept in the cool shade—home-brewed beer it may be or cold tea. Even these children, still too young to help bind, look eager and excited, for it is a great day for the labourers. Men are paid by the measure which they cut, not by time; and some have earned in one day, with wife and children to help tie, as much as fifteen shillings. A long day of English midsummer—from dawn to

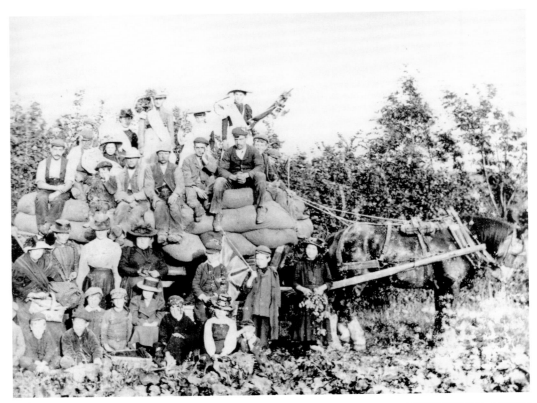

HOP PICKERS, ALTON

dark—may give fourteen hours of labour. All the rest of the year is ordinary routine from seven to five. The wage is not more than two shillings per day, often less, so the busy harvest weeks are fraught.

There are many companies of mowers in the field, for it must be done before night. Each reaper has his wife or daughters and boys to heap and bind, shirt sleeves rolled up, trousers belted and gartered, felt hats, necks and arms copper-brown and glistening, the shirts look blue, the corduroy trousers white or grey. The girls have fresh cotton frocks, white aprons, and all have the air of taking the work Joyfully like a holiday.

The young man, now beginning quite near me, rushes into his task like a swimmer breasting the waves. He plants his feet wide apart, grasps the scythe for a mighty sweep, and leans forward for the free swing of his arms. The wheat stands up to his face. With rapid, rhythmical strides and swinging arms he cleaves a path through the standing rustling corn, and as he forges on, breast deep, behind him lie eddies of silver and violet, still and motionless like the ripples printed on a sandy beach.

The men are displaying their strength and endurance for the admiration of wives and sweethearts. Even those who stand and wait are broiled in the sun, but the mowers stream with sweat. They often mop their brows, or eyes would be blinded. Now and then one calls for a drink, and a child, knowing the voice, runs out with a basket of provisions. It is thirsty work indeed.

Anna Lea Merritt

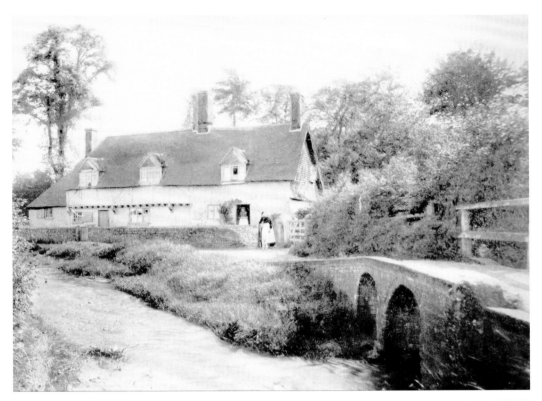

KETTLEBROOK COTTAGES, STEEP

HARVEST SUPPER

Old-fashioned farmers still give their harvest supper; but the new generation, without mutual hereditary interests between them and the labourers, disregard it. A general harvest feast for the entire parish has been tried; but to make it a success, there should be a thorough element of geniality and enjoyment in the entertainers.

The harvest feast in church is another thing. It is a modern invention, but is thoroughly enjoyed by the people, if they are encouraged to make their offerings in kind for the sick in hospitals. Very queer things come, and difficult to dispose of—enormous pumpkins, great pieces of honeycomb, apples enough to make the church smell like an apple-chamber, onions which have to be relegated to the porch, and big purple and white turnips, or long-tailed red carrots to be judgmatically disposed of.

Charlotte M. Yonge

A COUNTRY HOME

The house was originally a small farmhouse. It was about a hundred years old and built of the warm grey local stone. It stood on a little rise of a winding lane which ran at the foot of the steep sides of a vast raised plateau. The irregular sloping edge was in some parts bare like the downs; in other parts covered in a thick growth of tree—beech and yew for the most part—called hangars. . . . A large old-fashioned garden stretched in front of the house running parallel to the lane—and above it, for you entered the garden up half a dozen steps from the lane. . . . On the other side of the house the land sloped down to the stream which flowed through a wild water meadow full of forget-me-nots, meadowsweet, mares' tails and loosestrife. At night all we could hear was the wind in the hangar, the barking of foxes who lived there and the hooting of owls. It was a romantic and beautiful spot, and the house belonged to it and we loved it from the first.

Helen Thomas

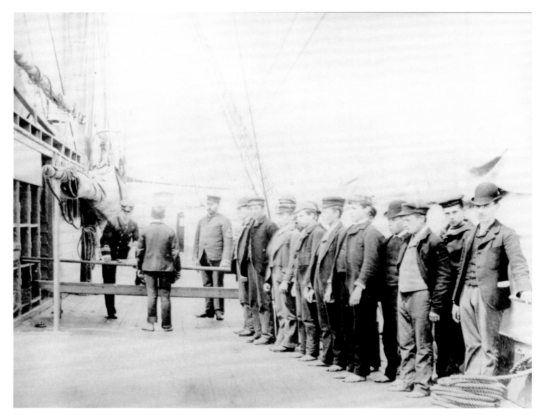

BOY RECRUITS ON BOARD SHIP, PORTSMOUTH

ARCTIC WEATHER

Early this morning Portsmouth Dockyard presented the appearance of an Arctic ice field. The ebb tide brought down an immense quantity of blocks of ice from the upper reaches of the harbour, and as they approached the entrance they extended right across from one shore to the other. The shallow water on either side was firmly frozen over. A large quantity of the drifting ice nearly filled the tidal basin, and the battleship Revenge, which is lying alongside one of the walls, was fast embedded in the ice. In this condition, she remained until the turn of the tide, at mid-day, when the ice broke up and drifted out. Several of the smaller basins in the Dockyard were frozen over, and the Portsmouth inner Camber was filled with ice. The harbour has not presented such an appearance for many years.

Hampshire Telegraph, 16 February 1895

WHITSUNTIDE WALK

Snowballs are among the delights of country childhood. To me they always recall the remembrance of the ecstasy it used to be to see the Whit-Monday procession of the village club, when the two tall banners, one of pink, the other of blue, glazed calico, were decked at the summit each with a peony and a snowball, and the Friendly Society 'walked,' as it was technically called. Each member carried a blue staff tipped with red, and had a blue ribbon round his tall hat, and almost all wore the old white round frock. The big drum was beaten lustily at their head, a few wind instruments brayed, all the rabble rout of the village stepped after them, and it was certainly a picturesque specimen of genuine village sports, perhaps the more so because the procession was, at the best, straggling and knock-kneed and often unsteady.

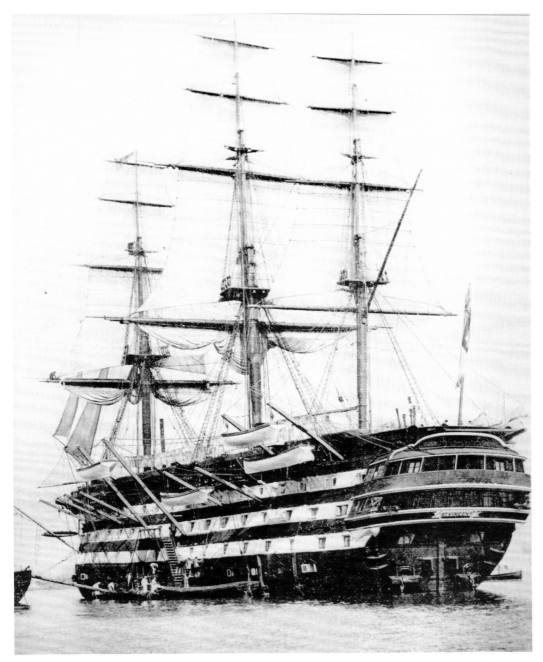

TRAINING SHIP HMS ST VINCENT, PORTSMOUTH

And oh! the odour of the church—a mixture of beery and tobaccoey human nature together with that of the fading young greenery of infant beech and larch boughs with which, even in those days, Whitsuntide decoration was kept up. Only very youthful and very rural nostrils could accept it as part of the festivity.

Afterwards there were banqueting and cricket on the village green upon the hill, and too much of that which was politely called 'breaking out at tide time,' popularly considered as a Saturnalia, not interfering with a character for steadiness and sobriety.

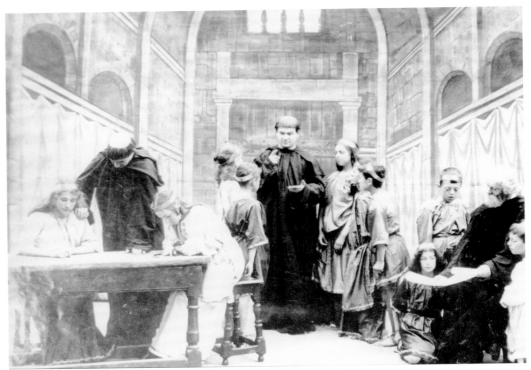

PAGEANT, WINCHESTER

At the present time, the prudent are divided between the Foresters, who, as every one knows, keep their great day with green banners and ribbons, in great numbers generally at the county town, and the County Friendly Society, whose carefully calculated tables they have become better able to appreciate, and which affords them a holiday, band, procession, and feast, much more decorous and civilised than their grandfathers would have relished.

This year Whitsuntide falls in June, but there is another May Day not to be omitted, namely the 29th, which for some unknown reason is called in Hampshire and Sussex, Shik Shak Day, and when those who omit the wearing of the oak-apple are liable to the drenching which in Devon belongs to the 1st.

Charlotte M. Yonge

FARMING

On Compton Farm never less than 20 horses were kept and about 20 men—more at haymaking and harvest-time and for root-hoeing. Farming, if somewhat leisurely, was very thorough, and weeds did not have much chance. A gang of 6 or 8 men still cut corn with the scythe, though reaping machines had appeared on the farm, but not self-binders. In those days it was not considered possible to get up hay with less than 14 to 16 people in the field, men, women and children. The field was all hand-raked and not a blade of grass left. On Compton Farm all the wagons and carts were made by Mudge the village wheelwright, and all the necessary ironwork, bonding of wheels, etc., was done on the farm. Mudge was a very fine craftsman. On Sundays every one went to church; the men always dressed in black coat and waistcoat made of very thick cloth and black bowler hats, a few of the older men still wore the old top hats. The women wore little black bonnets, and bright colours were taboo—to have worn flowers in your hat would have been almost indecent. The women did their shopping in Winchester; they walked there and back carrying their week's supply of groceries, etc.'

J. S. Drew

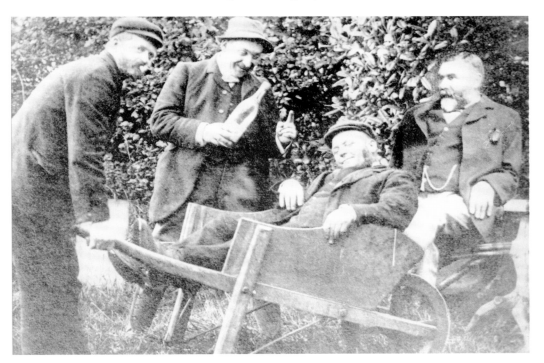

HEDGE END

HAMPSHIRE DRUNKENNESS

From a return just issued by the Home Office we take the following figures relating to drunkenness in Hampshire:—

Hampshire (County Council area) population, 352,817. The total number of persons convicted of drunkenness in 1895 was 1,039, of which 81 cases occurred on the Sabbath, between noon and midnight, and the remaining 958 at various other times. The total number of convictions in 1894 was 909, of which 10 cases occurred on the Sabbath and the remaining 829 at various other times. The total number of license holders convicted for permitting drunkenness on their premises, or for selling intoxicating liquor to drunken persons, was 20 in 1895 and 20 in 1894.

Portsmouth, population 159,278. The total number of persons convicted of drunkenness in 1895 was 414, of which 25 cases occurred between noon and midnight on the Sabbath, and the remaining 389 cases at various other times. In 1894 the total convictions were 385, of which 25 cases occurred between noon and midnight on the Sabbath, and the remaining 360 cases at various other times. The number of license-holders convicted for permitting drunkenness on their premises was two in 1895 and two in 1894.

Winchester, population 19,703. The total number of persons convicted of drunkenness in 1895 was 39, of which two cases occurred between noon and midnight on the Sabbath, and the remaining 37 cases at various other times. The total convictions in 1894 were 37, of which one case occurred between noon and midnight on the Sabbath, and the remaining 36 cases at various other times. The number of license-holders convicted for allowing drunkenness on their premises was two in 1895 and nil in 1894.

Southampton—population 82,126. The total number of persons convicted of drunkenness in 1895 was 348, of which 21 cases occurred between noon and midnight: on the Sabbath, and the remaining 327 cases at various other times. In 1894 the total number of persons convicted was 391, of which 21 cases occurred between noon and midnight on the Sabbath, and the remaining 370 at various other times. The number of license-holders convicted of permitting drunkenness on their premises, or for selling intoxicating liquors to drunken persons, was one in 1895 and two in 1894.

Hampshire Telegraph, 14 November 1896

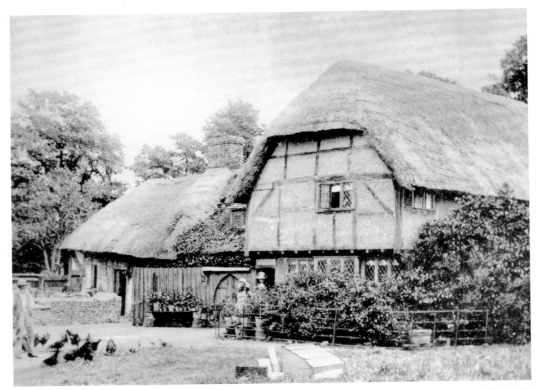

MONLAS COTTTAGE, HAYLING ISLAND

HAYLING FERRY

'It is a romantic spot, this Hayling Ferry. . . . It is only a very few hundred yards across from Hayling to Eastney, and yet the work of uniting has never yet been accomplished by bridge or American cargo boat. On the Hayling side is a little cottage and a little primitive inn, where the sailors going into the harbour congregate and drink good ale. On the Eastney side is another little cottage, surrounded with the "harvest of the sea", bits of anchors, hoops of barrels, old casks, wood, wreckage, enough old iron to stock a store, all cast up by the sea, and seemingly stacked here for years and years. I am told that this same Hayling Ferry has been in the same family for a generation, and on it goes, backwards and forwards, a long pull here, a strong pull there, with youth on one side of the ferry and old age on the other, just as it has done these hundreds of years. It is a bleak, wild, but not unfascinating spot. I have seen it in all weathers and all seasons, in midwinter and in mid-summer; and I like to sit down with "Jack" on the ale-house bench, as the wind whistles about our ears, and the peewits cry, and the sand-martins chase after the flies, and wonder whether the uniting of Hayling to the mainland will ever take place.

Clement Scott

WORKHOUSE INVALIDS

Sir,—Will you kindly allow me—in these fine days when flowers (garden and wild) are plentiful, and when flower services are being held, and picnics arranged—to remind your readers of the eight wards in the Union Infirmary, and of the great pleasure which flowers give there to both patients and nurses? I do not for a moment grudge flowers being sent to London, and of course our hospital ought to have some; but I would ask most earnestly that the old, infirm, and sick in our Workhouse should not be forgotten.

May I at the same time mention that in the Lean Department of St Thomas' Exhibition, to be held in the Parochial Hall, Southgate Street, next Tuesday, Wednesday, and Thursday, there will be one stall to exhibit the

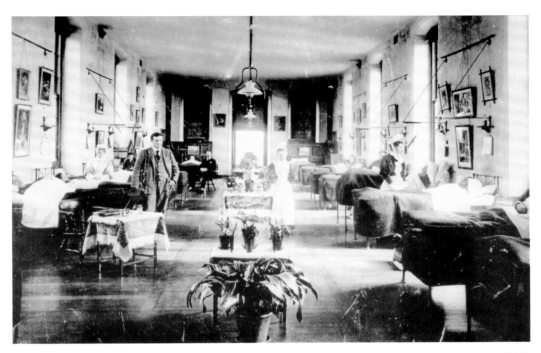

HOSPITAL WARD, WINCHESTER

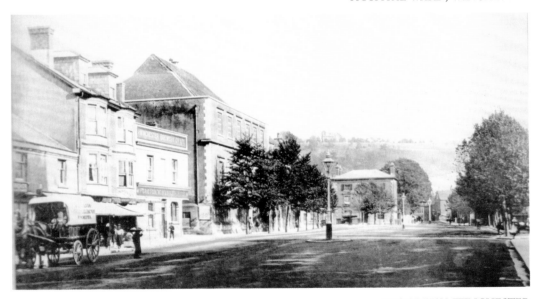

BROADWAY, WINCHESTER

articles made by the inmates of the Winchester Workhouse Infirmary, during the two months they have been taught under the Brabazon Employment Scheme. The exhibition is to be open daily from two p.m. to nine, and those interested in the poor invalids of the Workhouse are invited to pay their stall a visit.

I am, &c.,   A. R. Bramston.

Witham Close, Winchester, June 8, 1893

Hampshire Chronicle, 10 June 1893

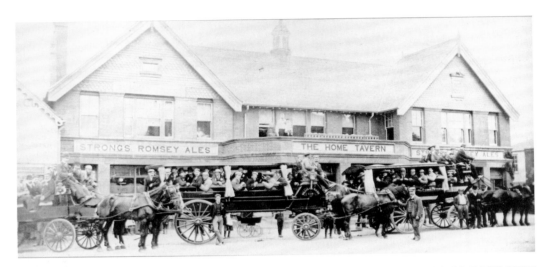

WORKMEN'S OUTING, EASTLEIGH

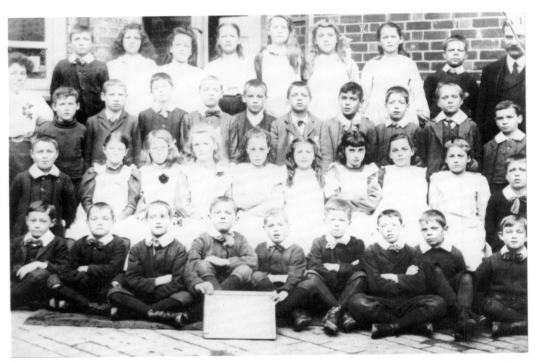

SCHOOL CLASS, WINCHESTER

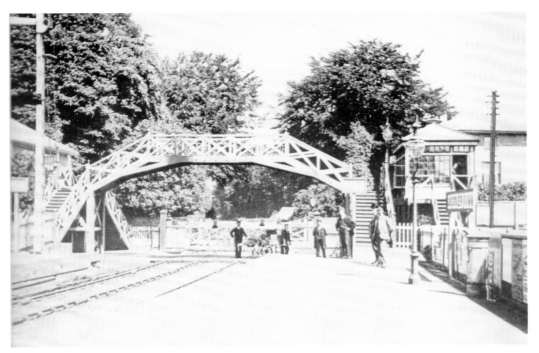

STATION, ANDOVER

EASTLEIGH

Time brings changes. Eastleigh was once a hamlet of Bishopstoke, now the latter is a village and Eastleigh a town. The station was at first Bishopstoke, but strangers confused it with Basingstoke, so it was changed to Eastleigh. In 1894 the railway carriage works at Nine Elms were removed to Eastleigh, and in 1910 the locomotive works. Eastleigh quickly grew into a town, the present population being approximately 20,000. The Church of the Resurrection, which Miss C. M. Yonge, the authoress, built in 1868 has since been enlarged three times by the additions of new nave, aisle and chancel. The Church of All Saints was built in 1910. It is, I think, well known that Miss Yonge's chief interests, and in which she spent the bulk of her earnings, were missions, education, and church building. The School-Chapel of Pitt was built by her. The children now go to Hursley School, and the folding doors within the altar rails, which formerly divided the School from the altar, are now folded back. The deep red tiled and yellow lichened roof is most picturesque, standing amidst the old heavily-thatched houses which make Pitt so attractive.

In 1896 there were a goodly number of the old villagers who gave the parish a rural atmosphere. They were chiefly attached to the large houses, and there was among them that air of dignity and respect and reserve which was very impressive and delightful to me after Kingsland in the Parish of Holy Trinity, Southampton, where so many down-and-outs sheltered till better days. It reminded me of the native village of my youth. There was a deep and keen sense of community among them. This was felt all the more when the eye; of the newcomers from London set their hearts upon the hill the other side of the water-meadows from the South-Western Railway Carriage Works and the River Itchen. At first land was not easily procured for building sites, but the lure of profit undermined every other consideration. The land between the Longmead southern boundary and the Fair Oak Road was acquired, and Hamilton Road (after the name of the purchaser of the land), Scotter Road and Guest Road (great names in the history of the S.W.R.) were soon built up; also Montague Terrace and the south end of Spring Lane and St Margaret's Road higher up the village. Later the land to the north of the Longmead Estate was in the market, and the old park-like field, the cricket field of 1896 lying to the east of the main village road, was largely covered with houses.

F. Dorothy Escombe

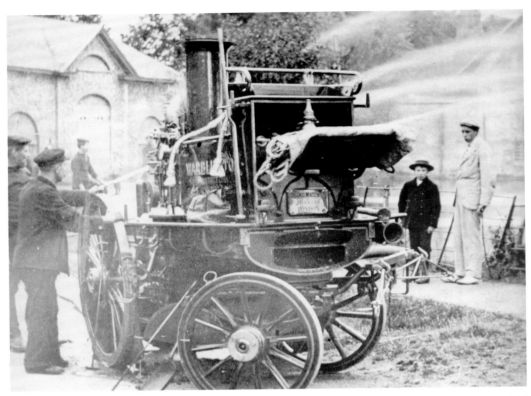

FIRE ENGINE, EMSWORTH

SERIOUS FIRE, MILE END

About 10 o'clock on Wednesday night some people passing 546, Commercial-road, Mile End, business premises in the occupation of Mr Alfred Hickie, oil, colour, and hardware merchant, noticed that the shop was filled with flames. At the same moment the plate glass front of the shop burst outwards with a loud report, and the flames and smoke belched forth across the pavement and far into the road. A tramcar stopped opposite the shop, the horses being startled by the flames, but the cries of the passengers, who feared that the car would catch fire, quickly caused the driver to proceed. Mr C. S. McFarlane, of the Kingston Brewery, who was on the car, at once proceeded to his office, and telephoned to the Town Hall that a serious conflagration was in progress. Mr McFarlane states that as the tram passed the shop and the flames shot out the passengers saw a man and woman rush out of the house and cross the road, the man carrying a child wrapped in a blanket sheet. A large crowd soon collected, and the neighbours were quickly apprised of the danger. Mr G. Moore, bootmaker, occupied the adjoining premises, Nos 548 and 550, using the ground floor as a shop, and the upper floor of 550 as a dwelling-house, and letting the upper portion of 548 to Mr Geo. Macy. Mr Moore himself was out, but Mrs Moore was just about to retire, and her nephew was actually in bed when one of the crowd tore off the handle of the front door in his attempts to awaken them to a sense of their peril. Mr and Mrs Macy, who were in their bedroom when the alarm was raised, quickly gained the street, where they met Mrs Moore and her nephew. Mr Dixon, cycle agent, of No. 544, also lost no time in vacating his premises and securing the safety of his family. Constables Watts and Ayton, both of whom were off duty, were among the first on the scene of the fire, and Watts immediately ran to the Regent-street fire-alarm, to find that the glass had just been broken by a young man who had seen the flare from a distance. Ayton made inquiries of the occupants of the adjoining houses as to the safety of Mr Hickie's family, and learning that the whereabouts of the nurse and child were uncertain, he went through one of the adjoining houses, accompanied by Mr J. W. Taylor (landlord of the Air Balloon, close by), and a bluejacket. They scaled several walls, and thus reached the back of the burning house. Breaking open

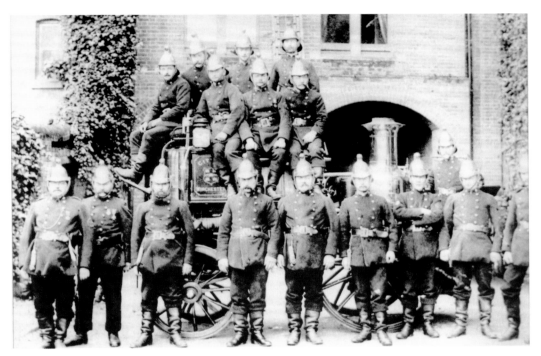

FIRE BRIGADE, WINCHESTER

the basement door they were driven back by the volumes of dense smoke, the house being already on fire from back to front. They were unable to penetrate more than a couple of yards, and could see no sign of any person in the lower part of the house. There was a blazing crate in the basement, apparently containing lamp glasses, and the policeman also saw what he took to be a barrel of oil blazing fiercely. They could only stay there a very brief time, and closing the back door, they returned to the front, where they met Mr Dewey, who had brought up the appliances kept near the Kingston Brewery. Constable Stares, in uniform, then arrived, ran out a hose, and with remarkable celerity got a jet of water to bear upon the front of the shop. This at once checked the flames, which had been creeping along the fronts of the adjoining houses. At about 10.15 a hose-reel reached the spot from the Buckland Police-station, and, under the direction of Inspector Brading, a second hydrant was got to work. The fire-escape from Lake-road shortly afterwards arrived, the crowd, which by this time numbered thousands, being somewhat facetious at the expense of the policemen in charge of the machine. Sarcastic inquiries were also made as to the whereabouts of the fire-brigade. Presently the two fire-engines came up at a gallop in charge of Superintendent Pordage, and a hose was carried through the premises of Mr Moore to bear on the back of the blazing house, while a fireman with another hose mounted a fire-escape, and directed a strong jet of water on the roof. The first engine was immediately set to work with deliveries from the front and back, but the services of the second engine were not required.

The shop occupied by Mr Hickie was gutted, and a part of the roof of Mr Moore's premises destroyed, considerable damage being occasioned to Mr Macy's furniture by the heat and water and the collapse of the ceiling. Unfortunately the loss is not covered by insurance. The stock and furniture of the lower parts of the building, occupied by Mr George Moore as a workshop, were also greatly damaged by water. The partition dividing the cycle shop from the burning building was burnt through, and the skirting boards right through Mr Dixon's house were scorched by the intense heat, the furniture being also much damaged. The loss sustained by Mr Hickie is only partly covered by insurance. During the evening Mr Hickie and his assistant had unpacked a case of wine glasses in the back room on the ground floor, and had left the case standing near the mantel-piece, on which was placed a common paraffin lamp. It is believed that in Mr Hickie's absence the lamp must have exploded and thus set fire to the premises.

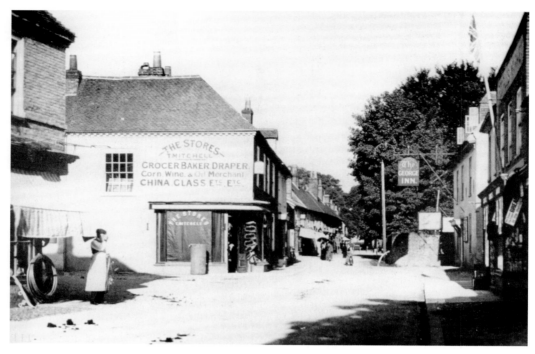

HAMBLEDON

The delay in the arrival of the Fire Brigade was due to an alarm received at 9.43 p.m. at the Central Station, where it was understood that the roof of Government House was ablaze. Both steamers at once turned out, in charge of Superintendent Pordage, who, on arrival, found that a tall chimney was on fire. The firemen experienced difficulty in reaching the chimney, which extended some 20ft above the roof, but the fire was eventually extinguished. At 10.14 p.m., just as the engines were preparing to return, information as to the outbreak at Mile-end was received from a police constable. The alarm had been received at the Town Hall about five minutes past ten o'clock from the Regent-street fire-alarm post, and Inspector Fry immediately sent a messenger to Government House to inform Mr Pordage of the circumstances. This message was supplemented by one from Mounted Police. Constable Harris, who galloped from the scene of the fire to inform the Brigade, and the two steamers immediately started with all possible speed for Mile End, passing the Town Hall at 10.12 and reaching the scene of the outbreak at 10.23.

Hampshire Telegraph, 8 September 1894

HAMPSHIRE PHRASES

Singing psalms to a dead horse, exhorting a stolid subject.

Sarplice, smock-frock.

'Ah! sir, the white surplice covers a great deal of dirt'—said by a tidy woman of her old father.

'And what be I to pay you?'

'What the Irishman shot at,' i.e. nothing—conversation overheard between an old labourer and his old friend, the thatcher, who had been mending his roof.

'Well, dame, how d'ye fight it out?'—salutation overheard.

CURATE. Have you heard the nightingale yet?

BOY. Please, sir, I don't know how he hollers.

Everything hollers, from a church bell to a mouse in a trap.

Charlotte M. Yonge

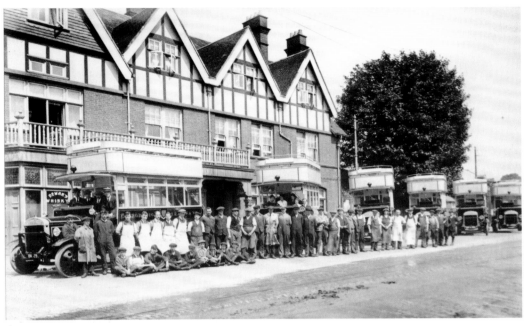

BUSES, WATERLOOVILLE

PORTSMOUTH MOTOR TRANSPORT

A motor bus licensed.—A unique application was made at the meeting of the Urban Sanitary General Purposes Committee on Wednesday, namely for a license for a motor bus to ply for hire in the streets of the borough. The motor, which is owned by a Brighton firm, is of a pleasing design, viz., much after the style of a large waggonette. The licence was granted. The motor bus, the motive power of which is petroleum, comes, we understand, under the Omnibus Act, and it will be restricted to a speed of eight miles an hour, and four miles an hour going round corners.

Hampshire Telegraph, 14 October 1899

WHEN FIRST

When first I came here I had hope,
Hope for I knew not what. Fast beat
My heart at sight of the tall slope
Of grass and yews, as if my feet

Only by scaling its steps of chalk
Would see something no other hill
Ever disclosed. And now I walk
Down it the last time. Never will

My heart beat so again at sight
Of any hill although as fair
And loftier. For infinite
The change, late unperceived, this year,

The twelfth, suddenly, shows me plain.
Hope now,—not health, nor cheerfulness,
Since they can come and go again.
As often one brief hour witnesses,—

Just hope has gone for ever. Perhaps
I may love other hills yet more
Than this: the future and the maps
Hide something I was waiting for.

One thing I know, that love with chance
And use and time and necessity
Will grow, and louder the heart's dance
At parting than at meeting be.

Edward Thomas

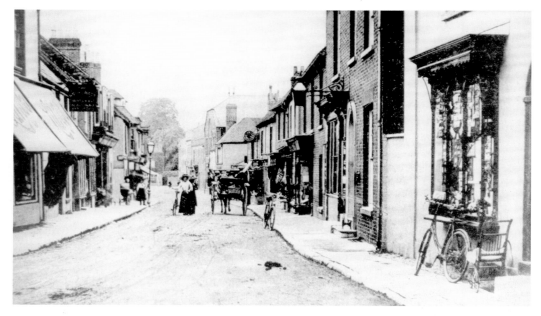

HIGH STREET, BISHOP'S WALTHAM

TRAVELS IN HAMPSHIRE

Royden House, Lymington, Hants,
July 5th, 1899?

DEAR ROBERTS,

Pardon long delay in answering your last, but I have been moving about a good deal. I got your note at Silchester, and went from there to Kingsclere, Overton, Whitchurch, and Andover—and then on to the forest. The Kingsdon part of the country is very fine, and the ride from that little town among the hills over high downs to the Test most beautiful. I kept along the Test to Romsey. From here I go on Monday to Rolestone,

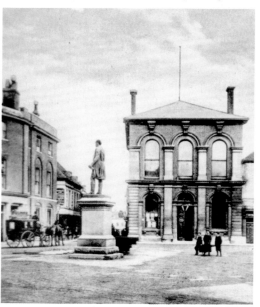

Fawley, Southampton, to stay till Wednesday, I think, and then if I do not return to town shall go over east to Bishop's Waltham, and Petersfield district and visit some of the villages and towns in that part, which I only partly know. Yesterday I spent the day at Milton with a naturalist parson, who has a lovely place, and is the leading authority on the natural history of the New Forest.

Of course you will be back in town now, and perhaps preparing for your excursion to the mountainous district of Europe. I hope you got good sport at Howtown and that Mrs Roberts enjoyed the visit.

With kind regards,
Yours ever,
W. H. Hudson.

W. H. Hudson

MARKET PLACE, ROMSEY

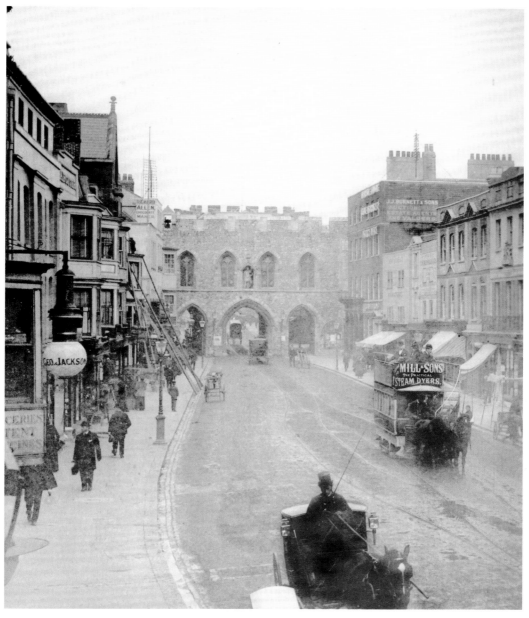

BELOW BAR, SOUTHAMPTON

HAVANT

Havant (a beastly hole), *Hants*,
April 15th (1900).

Dear Roberts,

I got yours yesterday morning at Petersfield. I came with Mrs H. on Wednesday last and we have been walking every day since in defiance of the furious cold winds. The curious thing is that we both had very bad colds when we left home and could hardly walk when we began our rambles, but day by day we have been getting better and are now pretty well. Between Petersfield and Harting we found a small pretty rustic village in a deep hollow among the downs.

W. H. Hudson

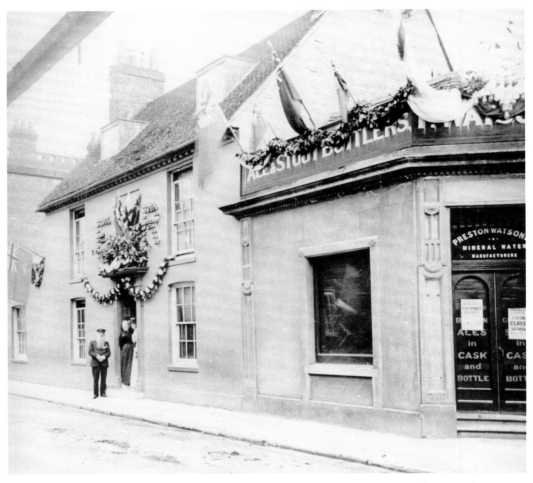

NORTH STREET, HAVANT

THE HUXTER

He has a hump like an ape on his back;
He has of money a plentiful lack;
And but for a gay coat of double his girth
There is not a plainer thing on the earth
    This fine May morning.

But the huxter has a bottle of beer;
He drives a cart and his wife sits near
Who does not heed his lack or his hump;
And they laugh as down the lane they bump
    This fine May morning.

Edward Thomas

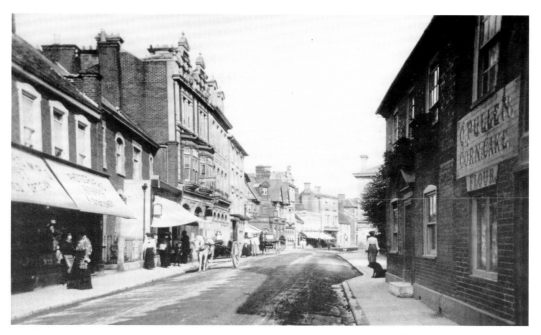

WEST STREET, HAVANT

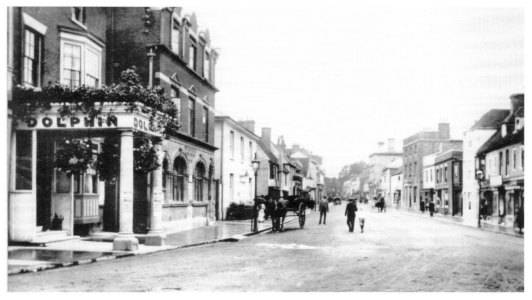

HIGH STREET, PETERSFIELD

THE ODD-JOB MAN

The man who lives under the roof and was born there seventy years ago is like his house. He is short and immensely broad, black-haired, with shaved but never clean-shaven face creased by a wide mouth and long, narrow black eyes—black with a blackness as of cold, deep water that had never known the sun but only the candle-light of discoverers. His once grey corduroys and once white slop are stained and patched to something like the colour of the moist, channelled thatch and crumbling 'clunch' of the stone walls. He wears a soft felt hat with hanging broad brim of darker earthy hues; it might have been drawn over his face and ears in his emergence

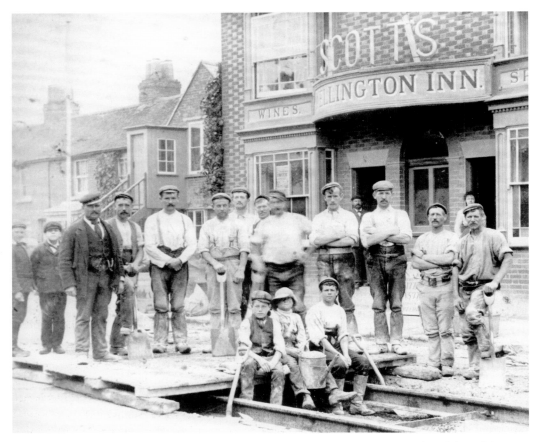

LAYING TRAM LINES, WATERLOOVILLE

from his native clay and flint. Only rarely does his eye—one eye at a time—gloom out from underneath, always accompanied by a smile that slowly puckers the wrinkled oak-bark of his stiff cheeks. His fingers, his limbs, his face, his silence, suggest crooked oak timber or the gnarled stoles of the many times polled ash.

That house he will never give up except by force, to go to workhouse or grave. They want him to go out for a few days that it may be made more weather-tight; but he fears the chances and prefers a rickety floor and draughty wall. He is half cowman, half odd job man—at eight shillings a week—in his last days, mending hedges, cleaning ditches, and carrying a sack of wheat down the steep hill on a back that cannot be bent any farther. Up to his knees in the February ditch, or cutting ash poles in the copse, he is clearly converted to the element to which he must return.

Edward Thomas

ARCTIC WEATHER

Portsmouth, in common with other parts of the country, has been suffering under a spell of the severest weather on record. The upper reaches of the harbour have been frozen over, and the thermometer has registered as low as 17 degrees Fahrenheit. Though greatly appreciated by skaters, who have been enabled to indulge in the exhilarating exercise to their hearts' content, we fear the weather has brought much suffering to the poor. In many cases the breadwinner has been thrown out of work, while in all the difficulty of obtaining sufficient firing, with coals selling at 25s. a ton, must have been very great.

One result of this Arctic severity has been the quickening of public sympathy for the little Board school children who, in too many cases, unfortunately are sent to school without having had sufficient food because

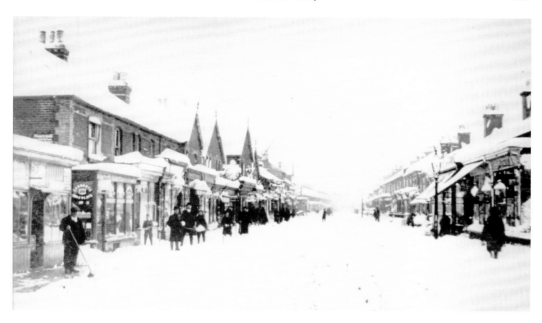

MARKET STREET, EASTLEIGH

of the inability of their parents to provide it. For these hungry little ones, the school staff prepare a warm and nourishing meal, the cost of which is defrayed by public subscription and the proceeds of the school concert, which forms one of the features of the school year in Portsmouth. All concerned in this truly charitable movement merit the warmest commendation, and we hope the public will respond as liberally to the appeal which has been made this week as the circumstances demand. Every morning some 800 children are fed, the severe weather having caused a considerable addition to the list of hungry applicants, and though the movement is conducted on the most economical principles, the inroads upon the fund have been so heavy that a speedy replenishing is most essential. We note with pleasure that on the recommendation of Councillor E. L. G. Foster, the Town Council has decided to let the School Committee have the use of the Town Hall absolutely free for three nights for the purposes of the annual concert. This is equivalent to a gift of £6 to the fund.

Hampshire Telegraph, 9 February 1895

THE LABOURER

> The thrush on the oak top in the lane
> Sang his last song, or last but one;
> And as he ended, on the elm
> Another had but just begun
> His last; they knew no more than I
> The day was done.
>
> Then past his dark white cottage front
> A labourer went along, his tread
> Slow, half with weariness half with ease;
> And, through the silence, from his shed
> The sound of sawing rounded all
> That silence said.

Edward Thomas

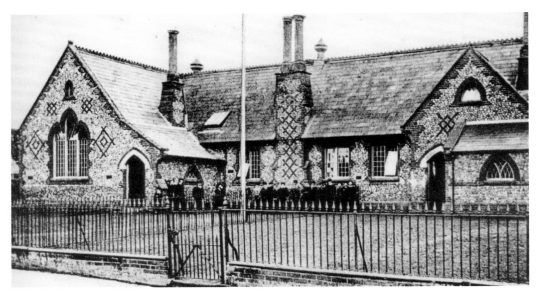

BRITISH SCHOOL, ANDOVER

EDUCATION

Technical education has, during the past year, been carried on in the County of Hampshire with, on the whole, most gratifying results. The director, Mr D. T. Cowan, has drawn up a voluminous report on the year's progress, and from it we gather that, taken as a whole, the classes were attended by those whom the instruction is desired to benefit, that the number of pupils was satisfactory, and that the failures were small in proportion to the successes. Amongst the subjects which have been taken up is one that should prove of much benefit to the poor in the neighbourhood of Botley, Swanwick, and Fareham. It is reported that this year Belgium had sent the enormous number of 50,000 gallon baskets to that district for use in the fruit industry, and with a desire of instructing local men in the manufacture of these articles classes were opened in the district. Despite the fact that the osiers with which the baskets are made have to be brought from a distance, the inclusion of this branch in the Hants curriculum of instruction appears to have been a wise proceeding. Referring to other subjects, we find that cookery classes are on the decline; very few of the dress-making classes have not been a success; interest in dairy work has increased; the Health Lectures have, on the whole, been satisfactory, but the woodwork classes have not yielded good results.

Hampshire Telegraph, 15 August 1896

SHEEP FAIR

The annual sheep and lamb fair took place on Thursday, and was in every respect the best that has been held here for many years. The fair ground on the Stockbridge road was occupied with an unusually large number of sheep, and both cattle and horses were largely in excess of the average. The trade was generally spoken of as good, recent prices being firmly maintained. The competition for prizes was exceedingly keen. The awards were as follows:—

For the best pen of wether lambs, 1st prize (£20), to Mr John Read, Downton, Salisbury; 2nd (£10), to Mr Frank Budd, Dummer, Basingstoke, 3rd (£5), to Mr George Judd, Cozum, Barton Stacey. For the best 100 ewe lambs for breeding purposes, 1st (£10), Mr Joshua East, Stockbridge; 2nd (£5), Mr Lyne, Compton, Winchester. For the best pen of lambs, any breed, open to farmers resident within the Hursley Hunt, 1st (£10, given by Mr A. E. Deane M.F.H.), Mr F. R. Hunt, Headbourne Worthy, 2nd (£5), Mr George Judd. For the best pen of lambs, any breed or sex, open to members of the Hants Yeomanry Carabineers, 1st (£10, given by the Earl of Airlie), Mr W. Allen Popham; 2nd (£5), Mr Westbrook, Corhampton. The customary pleasure fair was held in the town.

Hampshire Telegraph, 25 October 1890

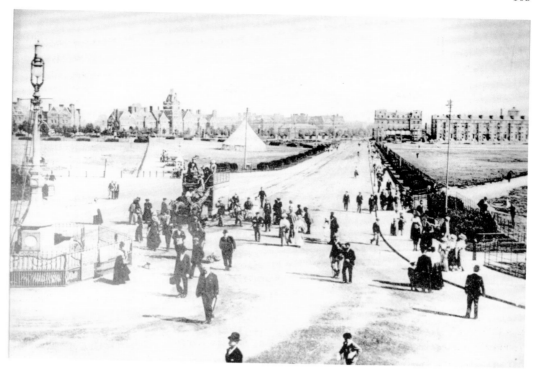

SOUTHSEA

BATHING

Those who love their morning dip off Southsea Beach are up in arms about a new regulation which has come into force entirely prohibiting bathing between the Castle and the New Pier, such as it has hitherto been the practice to allow before 9 a.m. It seems that the new order has been issued by the General Purposes Committee in consequence of a complaint received from a lady visitor who wants to walk along the beach in the early morning. Hundreds of men and youths who have been in the habit of hieing them to this fine stretch of beach for a matutinal dip are affected by the new and arbitrary regulation, and they are naturally indignant. It is to be hoped that the Committee, who, it seems, have absolute power in the matter, will see fit to revoke so drastic an order. Public authorities ought to encourage that cleanliness which we are told, is next to godliness, and—ungallant though it may be considered—we are fain to prefer the comfort and convenience of these male hundreds of residents and others who are affected before the caprice of an individual lady visitor.

Hampshire Telegraph, 23 June 1894

THE MANOR FARM

The rock-like mud unfroze a little and rills
Ran and sparkled down each side of the road
Under the catkins wagging in the hedge.
But earth would have her sleep out, spite of the sun;
Nor did I value that thin gilding beam
More than a pretty February thing
Till I came down to the old Manor Farm,
And church and yew-tree opposite, in age
Its equals and in size. Small church, great yew,
And farmhouse slept in a Sunday silentness.
The air raised not a straw. The steep farm roof,
With tiles duskily glowing, entertained
The midday sun; and up and down the roof
White pigeons nestled. There was no sound but one.
Three cart-horses were looking over a gate
Drowsily through their forelocks, swishing their tails
Against a fly, a solitary fly.

Edward Thomas

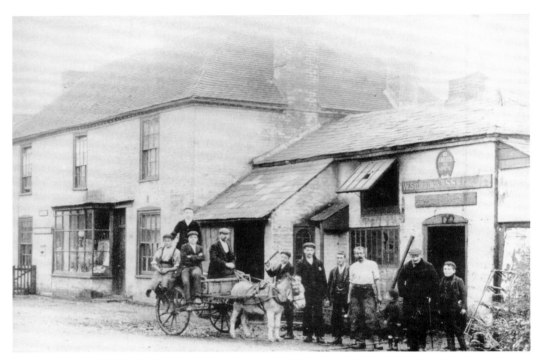

THE SMITHY, FAIR OAK

THE SMITHY

All day and night, save winter, every weather,
Above the inn, the smithy, and the shop,
The aspens at the cross-roads talk together
Of rain, until their last leaves fall from the top.

Out of the blacksmith's cavern comes the ringing
Of hammer, shoe, and anvil; out of the inn
The clink, the hum, the roar, the random singing—
The sounds that for these fifty years have been.

Edward Thomas

SUNDAY SCHOOL OUTING

About fifty years ago, Sunday School treats were occasionally taken to their destination in trucks, drawn by the local traction engine. One such treat went first to a village six miles down the valley for tea, and then the three packed trucks of excited children were brought home by way of the local market town, a hilly journey of some fifteen miles in all.

Another method of transport was by farm wagons lent for the occasion. The ponderous treading of the slow cart horses through the shady country lanes may seem dull and tedious to a generation used to motors, but the enjoyment was great. A start had to be made after an early dinner in order to reach the chosen destination in time for games before tea. Thirty or more boys and girls, with one or two teachers, clambered into each wagon, sitting on planks put across to form benches, or the older ones on the wide sides, or—a place of honour—beside the driver. A favourite place for such treats was Highclere Park, six miles off on the high northern slopes of the Downs looking over Berkshire. The road to it is a steady pull up for a large part of the way, through a narrow, very lovely and overhung lane, in which to pass anything involved complicated backing and manoeuvring, adding to the excitement of the youthful passengers. Next comes a stretch of woodland, and then out into the open till the southern slope of the Downs is crossed and Berkshire and Oxfordshire are seen spread out below. A rough track here turns through the park and leads to a lodge where teas were frequently provided under neighbouring beeches, and in front appeared the green sides of the hill which was the main object of such excursions.

Kathleen E. Innes

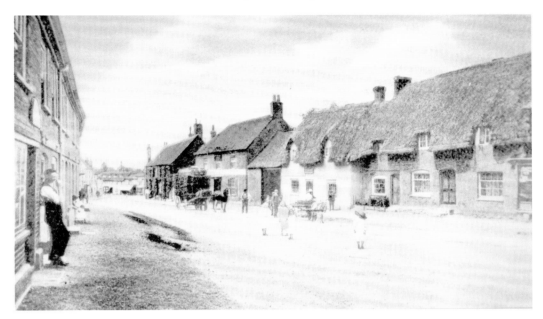

HIGH STREET, DOWNTON

MUMMERS

Christmas mummers still perambulate the villages, somewhat uncertainly, as their performance depends on the lads willing to undertake it, and the willingness of some woman to undertake the bedizening of them with strips of ribbon or coloured paper; and, moreover, political allusions are sometimes introduced which spoil the simplicity. The helmets are generally made of wallpaper, in a shape like *auto-da-fé* caps, with long strips hanging over so as to conceal the face, and over the shirts are sewn streamers.

Thus tramp seven or eight lads, and stand drawn up in a row, when the foremost advances with, at the top of his hoarse voice:

Room, room, brave gallants, room,
I'm just come to show you some merry sport and game,
To help pass away
This cold winter day.
Old activity, new activity, such activity
As never was seen before,
And perhaps never will be seen no more.

(Alas! too probably. Thanks to the schoolmaster abroad.)

Then either he or some other, equipped with a little imitation snow, paces about announcing himself:

Here comes I, Old Father Christmas, Christmas, Christmas,
Welcome or welcome not,
I hope old Father Christmas
Will never be forgot.
All in this room, there shall be shown
The dreadfullest battle that ever was known.
So walk in, St George, with thy free heart
And see whether thou canst claim peace for thine own part.

So far from 'claiming peace,' St George waves (or ought to wave) his wooden sword, as he clumps forth, exclaiming:

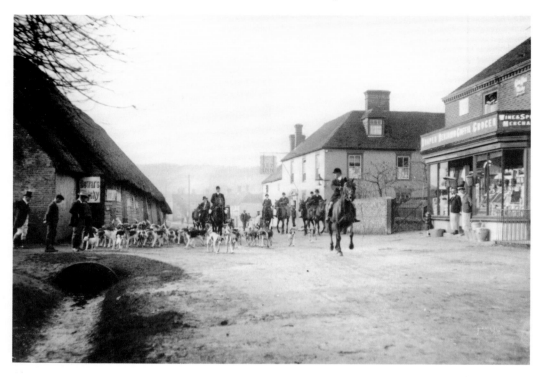

HAMBLEDON

In comes I, St George, St George, that man of courage bold,

With my broad sword and spear I won the crowns of gold,

I fought that fiery dragon,
And drove him to the slaughter,
And by that means I won
The King of Egypt's daughter.
Therefore, if any man dare enter this door
I'll hack him small as dust,
And after send him to the cook's shop
To be made into mince-pie crust!

On this defiance another figure appears:

Here comes I, the Turkish knight
Just come from Turkey land to fight;
I'll fight thee, St George, St George, thou man of courage bold,
If thy blood be too hot, I'll quickly make it cold.

To which St George responds, in the tone in which he would address a cart-horse:

'Wo ho! My little fellow, thou talk'st very bold,
Just like the little Turks, as I have been told,
Therefore, thou Turkish knight,

Pull out thy sword and fight,
Pull out thy purse and pay,
I'll have satisfaction, or thou goest away.

The Turkish Knight:
Satisfaction, no satisfaction at all,
My head is made of iron, my body lined with steel,
I'll battle thee, to see which on the ground shall fall.

The two wooden swords clatter together till the Turkish knight falls, all doubled up, even his sword, with due regard to his finery; and St George is so much shocked that he marches round, lamenting:

O only behold what I have been and done,
Cut and slain my brother, just the evening sun.

Then, bethinking himself, he exclaims:

I have a little bottle, called elecampane,
If the man is alive, let him rise and fight again.

The application of the elecampane so far restores the Turkish knight that he partly rises, entreating:

O pardon me, St George, O pardon me, I crave,
O pardon me this once, and I will be thy slave.

Very inconsistently with his late remorse, St George replies—

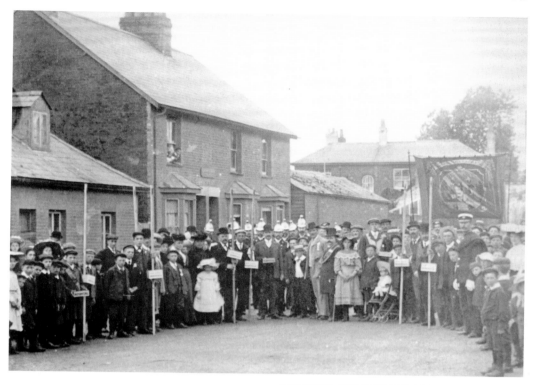

HOSPITAL SUNDAY PARADE, BEDHAMPTON

I never will pardon a Turkish knight,
Therefore arise, and try thy might.

The combat is renewed, and the Turkish knight falls prostrate, on which the Foreign King comes forward, shouting:

St George, St George, what has thou done,
For thou hast slain mine only son!

But, after marching round the fallen hero, he cries:

Is there a doctor to be found,
That can cure this man lies bleeding on the ground.

In response, the doctor appears:

O yes, there is a doctor to be found,
That can cure this man lies bleeding on the ground.

The anxious father asks:

Doctor, doctor, what is thy fee?

The doctor replies:

Ten guineas is my fee,
But ten pounds I'll take of thee.

The King answers:

'Take it, doctor, but what canst thou cure?'

The doctor's pretensions are high, for he says:

I can cure the ague, palsy, and the gout,
And that's a roving pain that goes within and out;
A broken leg or arm, I soon can cure the pain,
And if thou break'st thy neck, I'll stoutly set it again.
Bring me an old woman of fourscore years and ten,
 Without a tooth in her head, I'll bring her young again.

The king observes:

'Thou be'st a noble doctor if that's all true thou best talking about:
 And the doctor, taking to prose, replies:

I'm not like those little mountebank doctors that go about the streets, and say this, that, and the other, and tell you as many lies in one half-hour as you would find in seven years; but what I does, I does clean before your eyes, and ladies and gentlemen, if you won't believe your own eyes, 'tis a very hard case.'

The king agreeing that it is, the doctor goes to the patient, saying:

'I have a little bottle that I call golden foster drops. One drop on the root of this man's tongue and another

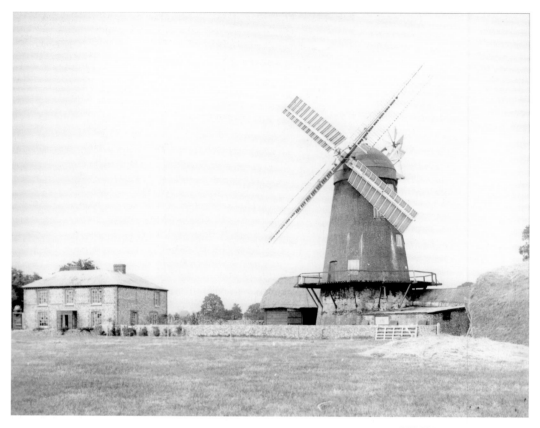

WINDMILL, DENMEAD

on his crown, will strike the heat through his body, and raise him off the ground.'

Accordingly the Turkish knight slowly rises and decamps, St George exclaiming:

'Arise, arise, thou cowardly dog, and see how uprightly thou can'st stand. Go home into your own country and tell them what old England has done for you, and how they'll fight a thousand better men than you.'

This last speech may have been added after the Crimean War, as the drama was copied out in 1857; but the staple of it was known long before, though with variations, in different villages, and it always concludes with little Johnny Jack, the smallest of the troup, with a bundle of dolls on his back, going round with a jingling money-box, saying:

> Here comes I, little Johnny Jack, Wife and family at my back,
> My family's large though I am small, And so a little helps us all.
> Roast beef, plum pudding, strong beer and mince-pies,
> Who loves that better than Father Christmas or I?
> One mug of Christmas ale soon will make us merry and sing;
> Some money in our pockets will be a very fine thing.
> So, ladies and gentlemen, all at your ease,
> Give the Christmas boys just what you please.

Charlotte M. Yonge

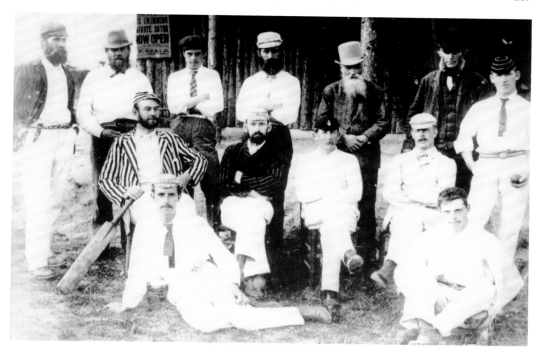

CRICKET TEAM, WHERWELL

HAMPSHIRE CRICKET

After having had all the best of matters, and showing superior form in every department throughout, Hampshire on Tuesday, at Southampton, inflicted a crushing reverse on Essex, to the extent of an innings and 61 runs. The latter county were twice disposed of for an aggregate of 221 runs, and except for some plucky batting by Burrell, McGahey, Owen, and Mead, the play calls for no comment. As a souvenir of his three consecutive scores of over a hundred, the County Club presented Captain Wynyard with a pair of handsome silver candlesticks, and Dr Bencraft announced that he had received many congratulations from counties and leading cricketers upon the excellent form recently displayed by Hampshire.

When the resolution of the MCC which admitted Warwickshire, Leicestershire, Essex and Derbyshire into the first-class ranks was carried, vigorous protest was entered by the supporters of Hampshire against the exclusion of that county. It certainly appears (says the Sportsman) as if those who raised their voices on behalf of Hampshire had good cause to do so, for undoubtedly the team have covered themselves with glory in the season which they brought to a close on Tuesday with a brilliant triumph over Essex, whom they defeated for the second time this year. For the first half of the season Hampshire could not manage to will a game, but since the beginning of August their career has been one of almost uninterrupted success, victories over Essex (twice), Derbyshire, Warwickshire, and Sussex having been gained since that period, while, in addition they had all the best of the drawn match against Leicestershire. After this brilliant record there is little doubt that Hampshire will be given a place amongst the first-class counties next season. Their win over Sussex was a complete triumph in every way, and it is worthy of note that they established a record in this match, for it was the only occasion on which a county has suffered defeat after declaring its innings closed. A glance at the batting table reveals a splendid record. Captain Wynyard's performance of scoring three successive hundreds is an occurrence which has rarely happened, and he comes out with the splendid average of over 66 for eight innings. Three others on the side also average over 40 apiece, and there are only six below 20. The attack, however, needs a great deal of strengthening, this being undoubtedly the weak point of the side.

Matches played, 11; won, 5; lost, 3; drawn, 3.

Hampshire Telegraph, 1 September 1894

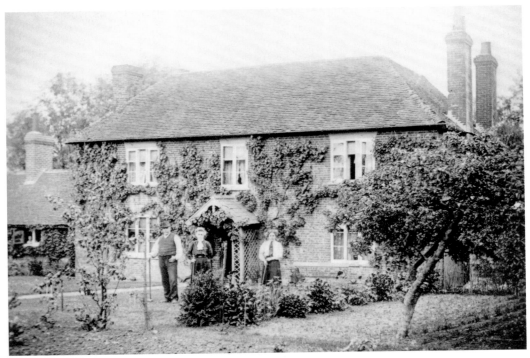

NORTH WARNBOROUGH

THE WAY TO PRIORS DEAN

The small village church with its low tower or grey-shingled spire among the shade trees, is beautiful chiefly because man and nature with its softening processes have combined to make it a fit part of the scene, a building which looks as natural and harmonious as an old hedge which man planted once and nature replanted many times, and as many an old thatched timbered cottage, and many an old grey ruin, ivy grown, with red valerian blooming on its walls.

To pull down one of these churches to put in its place a gigantic Gothic structure in brick or stone, better suited in size (and ugliness) for a London or Liverpool church than for a small rustic village in Hampshire, is nothing less than a crime.

When calling to mind the churches known to me in this part of Hampshire, I always think with peculiar pleasure of the smaller ones, and perhaps with the most pleasure of the smallest of all—Priors Dean.

It happened that the maps which I use in my Hampshire rambles and which I always considered the best did not mark Priors Dean, so that I had to go and find it for myself. I went with a friend one excessively hot day in July, by Empshott and Hawkley through deep by-roads so deep and narrow and roofed over with branches as to seem in places like tunnels. On that hot day in the silent time of the year it was strangely still, and gave one the feeling of being in a country long deserted by man. Its only inhabitants now appeared to be the bullfinches. In these deep shaded lanes one constantly hears the faint plaintive little piping sound, the almost inaudible alarm note of the concealed bird; and at intervals, following the sound, he suddenly dashes out, showing his sharp-winged shape and clear grey and black upper plumage marked with white for a moment or two before vanishing once more in the overhanging foliage.

We went a long way round, but at last coming to an open spot we saw two cottages and two women and a boy standing talking by a gate, and of these people we asked the way to Priors Dean. They could not tell us. They knew it was not far away—a mile perhaps; but they had never been to it, nor seen it, and didn't well know the direction. The boy when asked shook his head. A middle-aged man was digging about thirty yards away, and to him one of the women now called, 'Can you tell them the way to Priors Dean?'

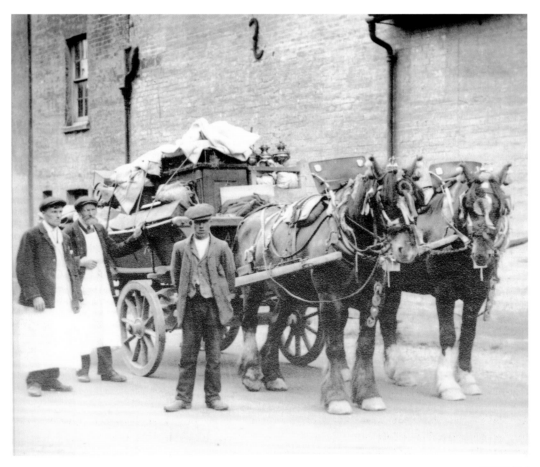

ODIHAM

The man left off digging, straightened himself, and gazed steadily at us for some moments. He was one of the usual type—nine in every ten farm labourers in the corner of Hampshire are of it—thinnish, of medium height, a pale, parchment face, rather large straightish nose, pale eyes with little speculation in them, shaved mouth and chin, and small side whiskers as our fathers wore them. The moustache has not yet been adopted by these conservatives. The one change they have made is, alas! in their dress—the rusty black coat for the smock frock.

When he had had his long gaze, he said, 'Priors Dean?'

'Yes, Priors Dean,' repeated the woman, raising her voice. He turned up two spadefuls of earth, then asked again, 'Priors Dean?'

'Priors Dean!' shouted the woman. 'Can't you tell 'em how to get to it?' Then she laughed. She had perhaps come from some other part of the country where minds are not quite so slow, and where the slow-minded person is treated as being deaf and shouted at.

Then, at last, he stuck his spade into the soil, and leaving it, slowly advanced to the gate and told us to follow a path which he pointed out, and when we got on the hill we could see Priors Dean before us.

And that was how we found it. There is a satirical saying in the other villages that if you want to find the church at Priors Dean you must first cut down the nettles. There were no nettles nor weeds of any kind, only the small ancient church with its little shingled spire standing in the middle of a large green graveyard with about a dozen or fifteen gravestones scattered about, three old tombs, and, close to the building, an ancient yew tree.

W. H. Hudson

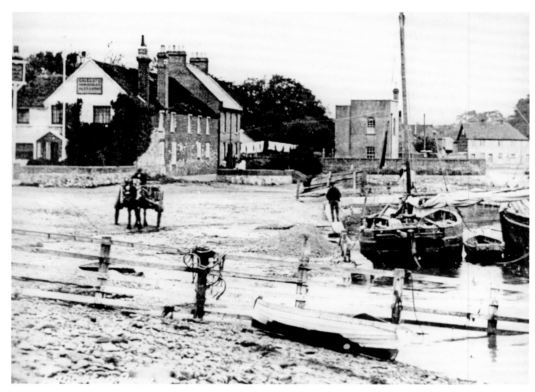

THE QUAY, LANGSTONE

PORTSMOUTH CANAL

What a long-standing monument of disappointed hopes and ruined fortunes the old Portsmouth Canal has been! Constructed nearly 70 years ago the promoters of it and shareholders in it anticipated great things, and in their dreams saw Langstone Harbour filled with shipping, and a constant procession of heavily laden barges going up the Canal to the centre of a thriving town. The awakening, however, was as rude as it was sudden. The Canal would not retain the water, and the traffic never came. The work and money had been absolutely thrown away, and until within the last few years the Canal served no other purpose than a playground for children.

Hampshire Telegraph, 7 September 1895

THE COMBE

> The Combe was ever dark, ancient and dark.
> Its mouth is stopped with bramble, thorn, and briar;
> And no one scrambles over the sliding chalk
> By beech and yew and perishing juniper
> Down the half precipices of its sides, with roots
> And rabbit holes for steps. The sun of Winter,
> The moon of Summer, and all the singing birds
> Except the missel-thrush that loves juniper,
> Are quite shut out. But far more ancient and dark
> The Combe looks since they killed the badger there,
> Dug him out and gave him to the hounds,
> That most ancient Briton of English beasts.

> *Edward Thomas*

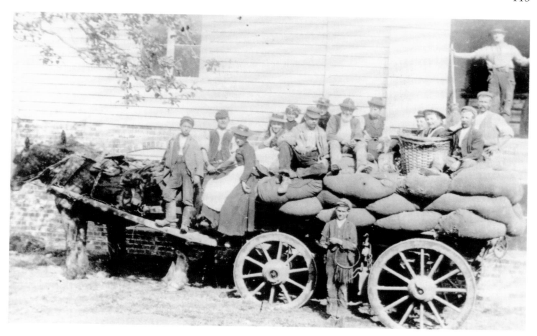

HOP PICKERS, ALTON

DEPRESSION AND FAIR RENTS

'Sir,—I had not meant to trouble you with another letter, nor should I have done so if Sir Walter Gilbey's hopes of the revival of agriculture and the reasons on which they are based appeared as satisfactory to me as they evidently do to him. These expectations are founded on the fact, which may be true, that 'the seasons during the past few years have been improving in comparison to the 11 years previous to 1865;' but, on the other hand, what have prices being doing during that time? During the last two seasons prices of agricultural produce have reached the lowest level ever known. It is not necessary for me to give details of the miserable prices to which beef and mutton, as well as wheat, have fallen; they are only too well known. Let there be the effect this coming harvest of the late great heat on the land that Sir Walter Gilbey anticipates, that, I maintain, is no assurance that the crops grown will realise better prices when placed upon the market. True, a good season is always better than a bad one, but what the agricultural community requires is a better value for their produce; they might then look upon an occasional bad season in a more even frame of mind, but now a bad season spells ruin to many men to whom with better prices it would only be a temporary loss and inconvenience.

'If a landowner is content for the future to receive £40 per annum for a farm for which but a short time ago he received £100, and a tenant is equally content to make 60 per cent less profit than he used to, then in some cases things may still run along, but neither those landowners nor those farmers can be said to have a prosperous time before them. With land taxed as it was in the days of protection, rates and taxes which always seem on the increase, tithe which in many cases is nearly as high as the rent, and in some exceeds it, agriculture cannot but continue depressed, but its depression is bound before long to make itself felt on other classes besides landowner and tenant, who at the present moment are between them bearing the whole burden. I do not believe that any country, and especially England, can afford to let its agricultural industry decline to the extent that we now see it in these islands without suffering grievously for it sooner or later, the millions of capital engaged exceeding by far the amount invested in any other industry in the country, and which is now earning nothing, or next to nothing, in an amount of wealth-producing power lying practically idle, and whose idleness is bound to be felt ere long. The fact that Mr Vancomer's report in 1795 shows things to have been worse then than now is not particularly cheering. In 1795 the British agriculturist had not got the whole world to compete against.'

Hampshire Chronicle, 13 January 1894

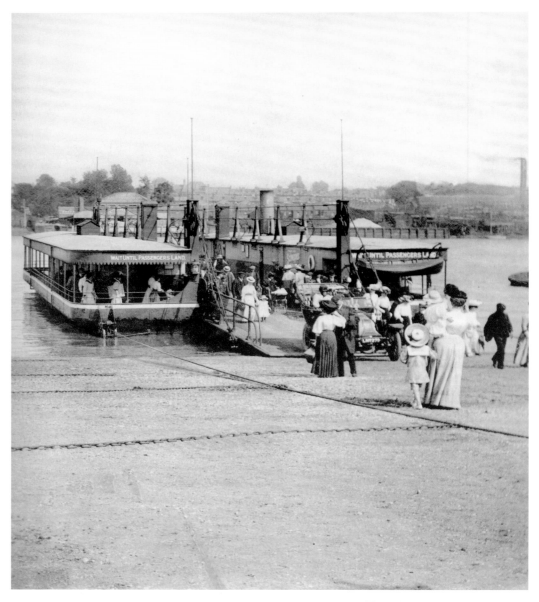

THE FERRY, SOUTHAMPTON

THE UNSEASONABLE WEATHER

Although we are now close upon Midsummer Day, the weather continues to behave in a most unsatisfactory manner, owing to the abnormal frequency with which shallow low-pressure areas follow each other from the Atlantic. Down to the end of April warm weather had prevailed all over the country for many weeks, but with May the conditions changed, and there has since been almost continuous cold, with dull, grey skies and frequent rain, the heaviest falls being in the east and north-east of England and Ireland, especially within the present month. In the 19 days ending at 8 a.m. on Wednesday Spurn Head had received over 4 in., the normal quantity for the whole month of June being only 1½ in. Donaghadee has had 4½ in., the month's average being under 2 in. Leith, Shields, York, Oxford, Yarmouth, and other places in the east have also had totals exceeding the normal for the month. For 50 days down to Wednesday the mean temperature of the Metropolis has been only 53 deg.,

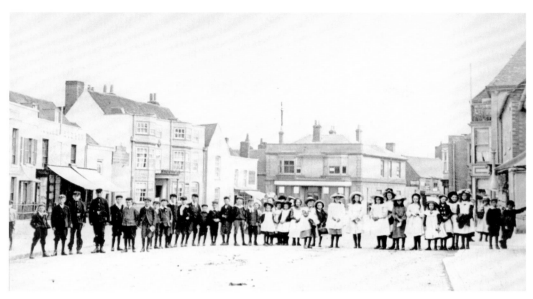

THE SQUARE, TITCHFIELD

against 59½ deg. for the corresponding period a year ago. The day temperatures have been unusually low, 70 deg. or 71 deg. being obtained only three times in seven weeks, while last year we had as many as 22 days with higher values than those—six of them between 81 deg. and 88 deg. A total of nearly 4 in. of rain, which has fallen on 23 days, is seven times as much as we had last year, when there were only ten wet days out of the 59. Bright sunshine has a very bad record, with a total of 210 hours, or a daily average of a little over four hours a day, against nearly perpetual sunshine in 1893.

Hampshire Chronicle, 23 June 1894

AGRICULTURE

In consequence of the decrease of the population, not only here, but in most rural districts, a vast impetus has been given to the use of labour-saving machinery on the farm. This has made quite a revolution both in the farm-yard and in the fields. The flail which used to be heard in the barn all the winter through, excepting Sundays, from six in the morning to five in the afternoon, is heard no more. The hum of the steam-thresher is no more foreign to the rustic ear than the cooing of the wood-pigeons, or the varied cries of the tenants of the farm-yard. In the wake of this machine others quickly followed—the grass-cutter and the reaper, which are employed on some farms to the exclusion of the scythe and the sickle. We have also been visited by the traction engine and the steam plough. With such helps as these at hand, real hard work has gone out of fashion, and the men and boys on the farms have an easy life at considerably higher wages than formerly. In 1852 the wages of an ordinary farm labourer were seven shillings a week, and now they are twelve shillings. Clothing of every description and all grocery goods are much cheaper, while bread and bacon—thanks to American importations—are about the same price, notwithstanding bad harvests. All this is against the farmer, and without any apparent benefit to the labourer or his wife and children who have no greater comforts than of old; perhaps the surplus finds its way into the pockets of the publican.

T. Hervey

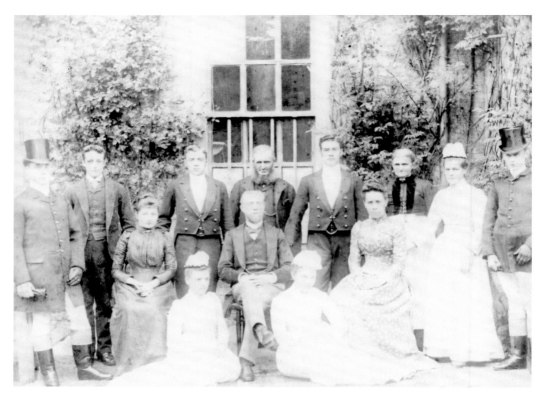

THE PRIORY SERVANTS, WHERWELL

ROUGH MUSIC AND MUMMERS

Another custom, which is in the realm of folk-lore, was practised within the last fifty years. It was known as 'rough music'. The latest occasion of its performance was a woman's desertion of her husband for another man. Several of the village men got together all kinds of instruments for making a noise, and went to the cottage where the guilty couple were living and 'performed'. The racket made so convinced the pair of the disapproval of their neighbours that they left the place for the nearby town. The story had a tragic sequel, for the deserted husband hanged himself.

One more very old custom connected with Christmas survived till well over the beginning of this century, but seems now to have disappeared. It was that of Mummers, in clothes decked with paper streamers, curious hats and wooden weapons, who called at houses and performed a play of St George's exploits and combats in the East, the story of which was mingled with nature legends of the turn of the seasons, the wording, learnt by heart, being in places quite unintelligible.

Kathleen E. Innes

THE VILLAGE IN WINTER

The New Year is coming in! Here, in South Hampshire, Christmas does not often come in conventional form, laden with snow. 'As the day lengthens, the cold strengthens,' is a very true proverb, but the lengthening is seldom perceptible till after Twelfth Day, and it is well for the poor that the severest weather should not often set in till there is a little less darkness. When I first remember the families used to go to bed as soon as the father had come in, so as to save fire and candle; but better wages and paraffin have made a difference, and each cottage shows a cheerful light over its muslin blind, with the geraniums that flourish so wonderfully behind it. These years have done much every way for the labourers' families. The dark blue cotton, sprung from 'Nancy Peel's'

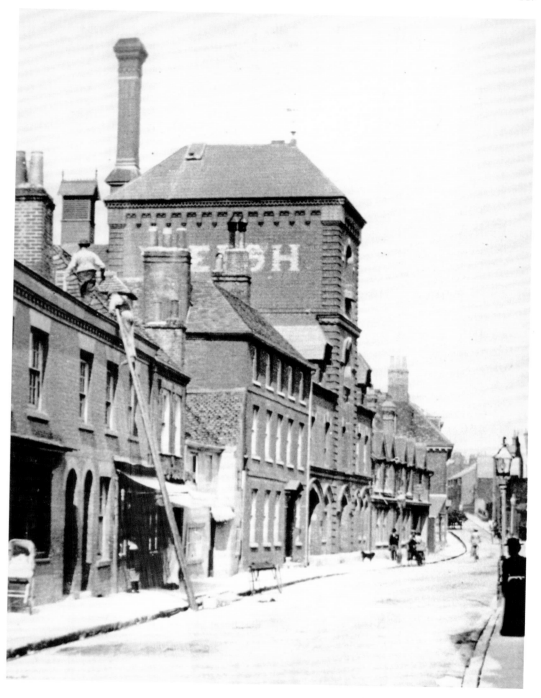

HYDE STREET, WINCHESTER

parsley pattern, has given place to the serge, too often, indeed, shoddy, but warmer and less liable to catch fire; and short sleeves no longer expose brawny arms and blue elbows.

This is the worst month, however, for work, especially for the brickmakers, who are numerous.

Charlotte M. Yonge

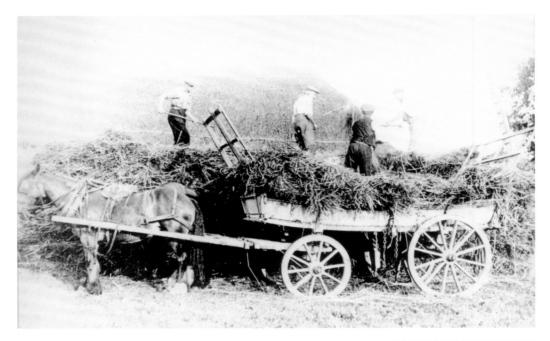

RICK BUILDING, BOTLEY

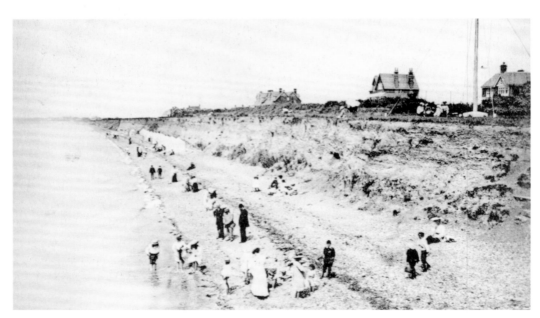

LEE-ON-THE-SOLENT

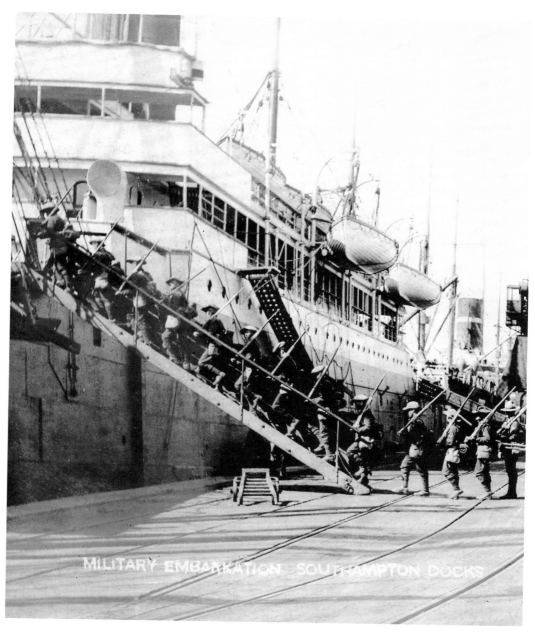

MILITARY EMBARKATION SOUTHAMPTON DOCKS

TROOPS EMBARKING FOR SOUTH AFRICA ON A UNION CASTLE LINE SHIP FROM
SOUTHAMPTON DOCKS C.1905.

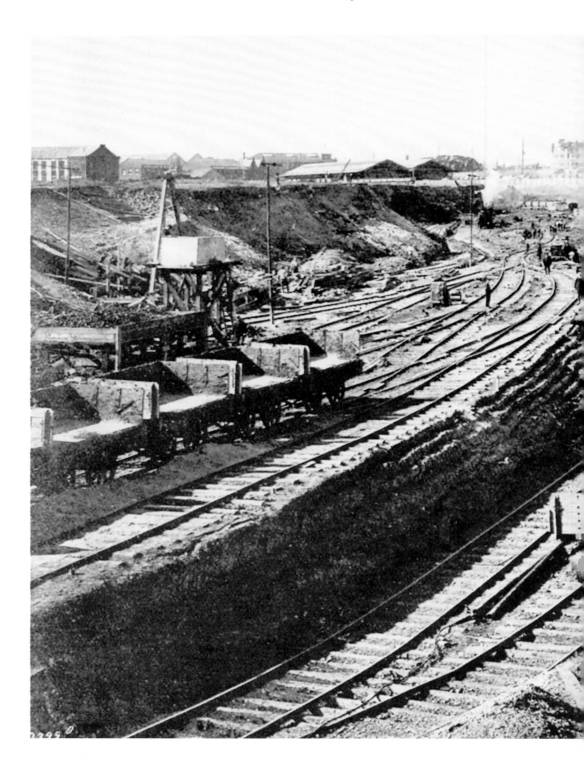

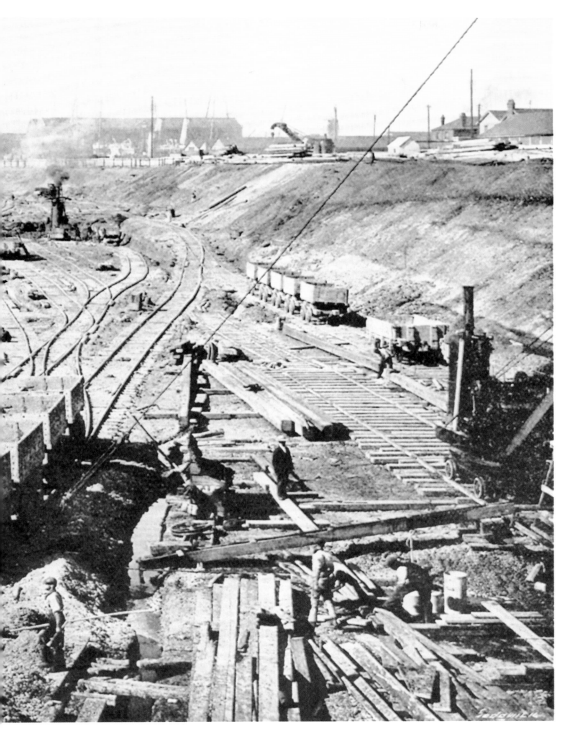

EXCAVATION WORK FOR NEW DOCK, JUNE 1908

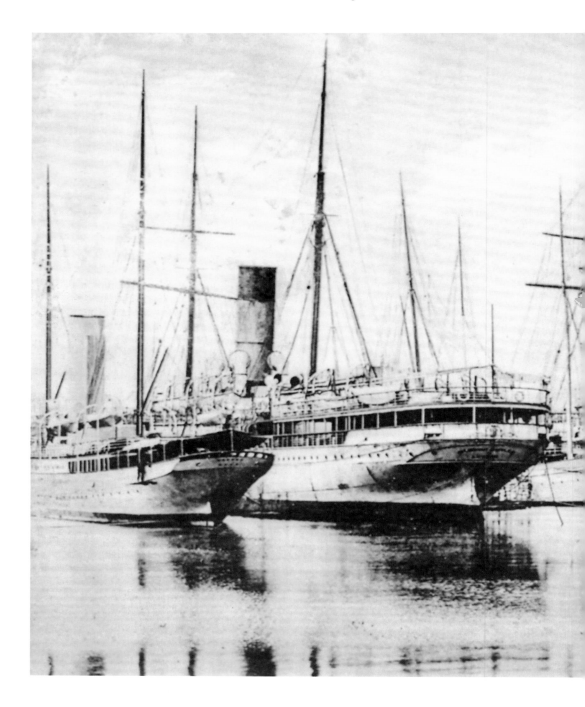

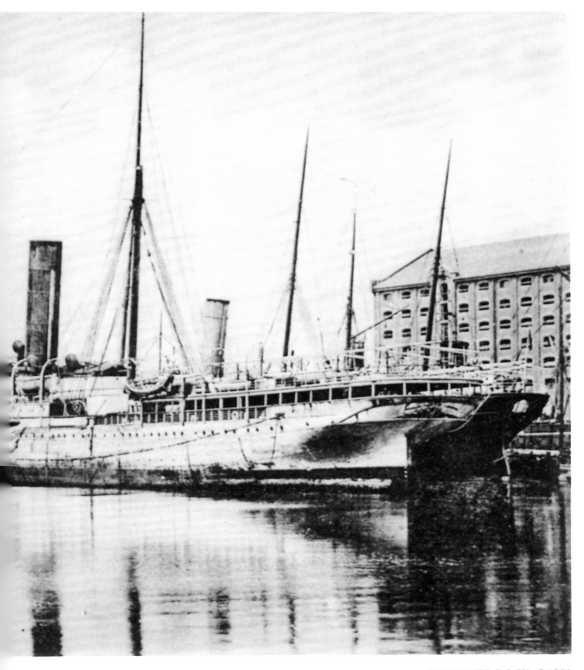

THE INNER DOCK, C.1900

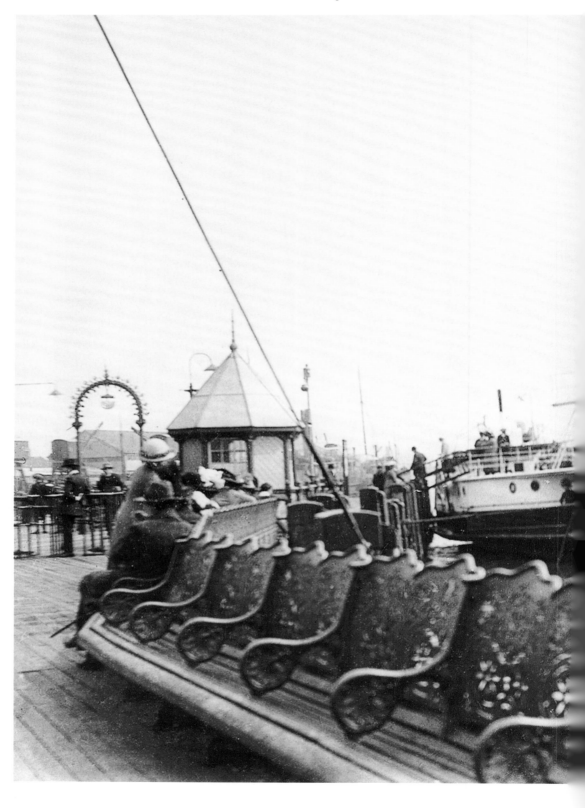

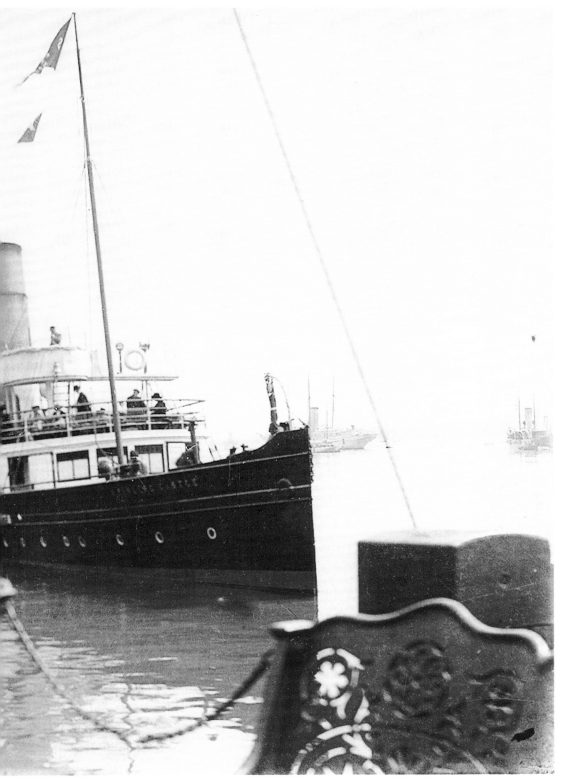

PS *STIRLING CASTLE* AT THE TOWN QUAY, C.1910

SOURCES AND PHOTOGRAPHS

TEXT

The page numbers given below relate to pages in this book and not the page numbers of the source books.

Sources of the text are as follows: WW Capes *Rural Life in Hampshire*; J.S. Drew *Compton, near Winchester*; F Dorothy Escombe *Bygone Bishopstoke*; Winifred Griffiths *One Woman's Story*; T. Hervey *A History of Colmer and Priors Dean*; WH. Hudson *Hampshire Days, Men, Book, and Birds*; Kathleen E. Innes *Life in a Hampshire Village*; Anna Lea Merritt *A Hamlet in Old Hampshire*; Clement Scott *A Rainy Summer on Hayling Island*; T.W Shore *A History of Hampshire*; Edward Thomas *Collected Poems, The South Country*; Helen Thomas *from* Jan Marsh *Edward Thomas: A Poet for his Country*; Charlotte M. Yonge *An Old Womans's Outlook*; John Kebble's Parishes: *A History of Hursley and Otterbourne*.

Newspapers Include *Hampshire Chronicle*; *Hampshire Telegraph*.

ILLUSTRATIONS

The illustrations are reproduced by kind permission of Hampshire County Library, except for the following page numbers, 10, 19, 21, 28, 34, 40, 74, 80, 85, 86, 104, 111, 112: these are taken from the author's collection.